UNIVERSITY OF NORTH CAROLINA AT CHAPEL HILL
DEPARTMENT OF ROMANCE LANGUAGES

NORTH CAROLINA STUDIES
IN THE ROMANCE LANGUAGES AND LITERATURES

Founder: URBAN TIGNER HOLMES

Distributed by:

UNIVERSITY OF NORTH CAROLINA PRESS
CHAPEL HILL
North Carolina 27514
U.S.A.

NORTH CAROLINA STUDIES IN THE
ROMANCE LANGUAGES AND LITERATURES

Number 215

CECCO ANGIOLIERI

A STUDY

CECCO ANGIOLIERI

A STUDY

BY
GIFFORD P. ORWEN

CHAPEL HILL
NORTH CAROLINA STUDIES IN THE ROMANCE
LANGUAGES AND LITERATURES
U.N.C. DEPARTMENT OF ROMANCE LANGUAGES
1979

Library of Congress Cataloging in Publication Data

Orwen, Gifford Phillips, 1910-
  Cecco Angiolieri.

  (North Carolina studies in the Romance languages and literatures; no. 215)
  Bibliography: p.
  1. Angiolieri, Cecco, ca. 1258-ca. 1312—Criticism and interpretation.
I. Series.
PQ4265.A6207   851'.1   79-21049
ISBN 0-8078-9215-7

I.S.B.N. 0-8078-9215-7

DEPÓSITO LEGAL: V. 2.332 - 1979   I.S.B.N. 84-499-3086-3
ARTES GRÁFICAS SOLER, S. A. - JÁVEA, 28 - VALENCIA (8) - 1979

CONTENTS

	Page
PREFACE	9
NOTE ON TRANSLATIONS	11
INTRODUCTION	13

CHAPTER

		Page
I.	SIENA AND ANGIOLIERI	21
II.	THE SONNETS	29
	a) The Becchina Cycle	29
	b) Money Themes and Family	44
	c) Incidental Themes	60
	d) Sonnets of Dubious Attribution	69
III.	STYLE AND TECHNIQUE	83
SELECTED BIBLIOGRAPHY		101

PREFACE

The section "Sonnets of Dubious Attribution" appeared in slightly modified form in the 1974 Winter issue of *Italica* (Vol. 51, Number 4). I should like to express my thanks to the Journal for permitting me to use the material again in my present study.

GIFFORD P. ORWEN

PREFACE

NOTE ON TRANSLATIONS

Most of the translations provided come from the pens of three gifted writers, Dante Gabriel Rossetti, C.H.M.O. Scott, and Thomas Caldecott Chubb. It would be difficult to sustain logically a preference for one as against another. The choice I have made in the case of a given sonnet is entirely personal, even fortuitous. Where no credit is indicated, the translation is my own. In these latter there is no pretence at the artful. I have merely endeavored to convey the meaning and suggest the tone of the original. My efforts might be termed "informational." They make no claim to touch those of the aforementioned poets. Their only virtue is that the quality of the language is, I feel, somewhat more in keeping with that of Angiolieri.

The entire question of translation insofar as this extraordinary Italian is concerned deserves further comment. His verbal gymnastics, the marvelous dash of the rhythms, his complete technical mastery, the piquancy of his sallies, and the topical allusions tend to elude a gifted, let alone average, translator. It is virtually impossible to render the total effect of his verse. With poetry of the aulic school, greater fidelity can be obtained; with Angiolieri this is not the case. His language is essentially a subtle blend of the colloquial with the learned, rendered by an artist who is a splendid showman to boot. The sonnets were for recitation rather than reading with the result that the auditive aspect is of great importance. The effects are studied; the pyrotechnics oftentimes vertiginous. One simply cannot convey this totality from one tongue to another. If one aspect is accurately caught, another is slighted.

His first translator, Dante Gabriel Rossetti, who included some 20 of Cecco's sonnets in his *Early Italian Poets* published in London in 1861, provides versions that are eminently fair to Angiolieri. Though a patina of Victorian propriety and reserve prevail — he notes, for example, after one translation, "I have thought it necessary to soften one or two expressions in the sonnet" — in general, he tampers very little with the language. Present-day scholarship would dispute an occasional interpretation, but essentially his renderings are admirable.

A special word of praise is long due C.H.M.D. Scott whose *Sonnets of Cecco Angiolieri Done into English Doggerel*, Chiswick Press, London, 1925, was unfortunately printed only for private circulation. His use of the word "doggerel" with its denigratory connotations is unfortunate because these are remarkably felicitous renderings. Mr. Scott is a true poet who has been at great pains to preserve with rare fidelity what Angiolieri said. He has done so in what might be termed apt and graceful rimes, but he plays Angiolieri false in sanitizing his language, as it were. The racy guttiness and vulgarity have disappeared. The translations are *ad usum delphini*, and inevitably a product of their time. Much the same might be said for the fine translation published in 1970 by the distinguished student of Italian letters, Thomas Caldecott Chubb. Mr. Chubb, too, is a first-class poet who catches remarkably well the brio and movement of Cecco's verse, but in a language which remains essentially a little too courtly and elegant. Interestingly enough, Cecco's language would seem to have a close affinity with American English of today. Perhaps some bold young translator of talent will again essay the task.

Even though the reader has a knowledge of Italian, the accompanying English versions will, I trust, serve to guide him past archaic forms and clarify Cecco's propensity for elision and apocopation which can be rather baffling at times.

INTRODUCTION

During the past century Italian scholars have found in the enigmatic Cecco Angiolieri an intriguing subject for speculation. The Sienese poet occupies, in a sense, a unique position in Italian letters. His literary production approximately equals that of José-Maria de Hérédia — to wit, a hundred and some sonnets. Yet it has elicited a corpus of critical commentary and exegesis which, in proportion to his slim output, is comparable to that accorded writers of the magnitude of Leopardi and Manzoni. To the general reader, Angiolieri is known because of three or four fulminating sonnets which find their way into all standard anthologies. His bland admission that three things alone appeal to him: women, the tavern and gambling, his reputation as a cynical wastrel and pederast, his hearty and unmitigated abomination of his parents, his anguished pursuit of the sluttish wife of another, and the similarities which he bears to Villon and Rutebeuf have invited continuing interest. Many have pursued his elusive image, and the diversity of reaction only attests to a certain durable attraction which this strange iconoclast never fails to exercise.

How many epithets he has borne! For Crescimbeni he was a "poeta facetissimo."[1] Others including Quadrio (1741) and Mazzucchelli (1753) merely echo this convenient appellation.[2] Trucchi, however, in his *Poesie Italiane Inedite de Dugento Autori,* offers, as it were, a breakthrough in recognizing in Cecco, "una nova,

---

[1] "a most facetious poet" Giovanni Mario dei Crescimbeni, *L'Istoria della Volgar Poesia* (Roma, 1698), p. 262.

[2] Vid. Fernando Figurelli, *La Musa Bizzarra di Cecco Angliolieri* (Napoli, 1950), p. 271.

scellerata ed empia, ma energica maniera di poetare."[3] For Bartoli, he is "il povero Cecco... che piange cogli occhi, mentre ride colla bocca."[4] For Papini he represents the "stizzosa lepidezza dei diavoli dell' Inferno."[5] Almost contemporaneously, Flora in his severe essay characterizes him as "questo poeta reprobo e maladetto" and "l'insofferente Cecco."[6] More recently Figurelli, Sapegno and Marti, among others, have offered more substantial and measured appraisals, weighing judiciously factors of historicity, psychology and intuition against a careful consideration of the sonnets themselves.

Curiously enough, in spite of the lively interest which Angiolieri has elicited among his compatriots, he has been almost entirely neglected by foreigners. Probably the first to note his talent was the not completely foreign Dante Gabriel Rossetti in his *The Early Italian Poets*,[7] in which he offers some remarkably apt translations and a short essay of interest. The entire *Canzoniere* was translated in 1925 by C.H.M.O. Scott in a very small and privately distributed edition. The author modestly and quite inappropriately terms his renditions "English doggerel." They are, on the contrary, very accurate and very felicitous translations whose only shortcoming is that they fail to reflect the pithy vulgarity of Angiolieri; but apart from this they reveal the craftsmanship of an extremely gifted translator.[8] Within the last fifteen odd years, sporadic interest in the poet has been evinced in various quarters. Twelve of the better known sonnets were made available in Dutch with a short introductory note by W. van Elden,[9] as well as an estimable study, *Cecco en de anti-Beatrice* by Herman van den Bergh.[10] An article in German by Hans Rheinfelder was devoted largely to Angiolieri,

---

[3] "a new, villanous and wicked but energetic way of versifying" Francesco Trucchi, Op. cit. (1846), p. 271.
[4] "Poor Cecco... who weeps with his eyes, but laughs with his mouth," Adolfo Bartoli, *La Poesia Italiana nel Periodo delle Origini* (Firenze, 1879), p. 269.
[5] "the spiteful wit of the devils of hell" Giovanni Papini, *Storia della Letteratura D'Itlia* (Firenze, 1937), p. 113.
[6] "that odious and reprobate poet... the unsufferable Cecco" Francesco Flora, *Storia della Letteratura Italiana* (Milano, 1945), I, p. 94.
[7] Dante Gabriel Rossetti, *Op. cit.* (London, 1861).
[8] Cecco Angiolieri, *Sonnets Done in English Doggerel,* trans. C.H.M.O. Scott (London, 1925). One of 30 copies for private distribution.
[9] W. van Elden, "Cecco Angiolieri," *De Gids,* VIII/IX (1957), pp. 75ff.
[10] Herman van den Bergh, *Cecco en de Anti-Beatrice* (Gronigen, 1963).

but as its title indicates, deals with references to health and healing in 13th century Italian poetry, and is thus of rather limited scope.[11] With the exception of a fine translation of the *Canzoniere* in 1970 by the distinguished American scholar, Thomas Caldecot Chubb, little else is encountered in the realm of foreign scholarship.[12] The task of rediscovering and interpreting Angiolieri has thus remained substantially in Italian hands.

Basic to any valid appraisal of the poet has been the establishing of a definitive edition of his work. This has proven a formidable undertaking. Even today, uncertainties in the ascription of some of the sonnets have left gray areas in which criticism can be little more than guarded conjecture. Cecco was first known to the reading public through the collection of a Monsignor Allacci, *Poeti Antichi raccolti dai Codici Manoscritti della Biblioteca Vaticana e Barberiniana,* Napoli, 1661, which presented a mere 30 sonnets. Apart from the important essay of d'Ancona in 1874, which re-established Cecco in the history of Italian letters,[13] no further work of significance was accomplished in this area until the present century when Francesco Massera published his collection of some 150 sonnets.[14] Primary sources of his compilation consist of approximately 30 manuscripts, of which the most important is the *Chigiano* L. VIII, 305, of the 14th century. The ultimate selection was drawn from eleven of these, considered by Massera to be basic. The deciphering of the codices, in itself a thorny task, was further complicated by the presence of a number of anonymous poems sufficiently in the tone and workmanship of Angiolieri to pass muster. Some were assumed to be re-workings, or alternate versions of the poet himself, others the work of imitators. A quarter of a century

---

[11] Hans Rheinfelder, *Lebensvorgänge, Krankheiten und Heilung in en Gedichten* Cecco Angilier's und anderer burlesker Dichter der Dantezeit (München, 1960).

[12] Thomas C. Chubb, *The Sonnets of a Handsome and Well-Mannered Rogue* (Hamden, Conn., 1970).

Also vide: "El Antistilnovismo de Cecco Angiolieri" Montevideo Universidade, Humanidades y ciencias Faculdade, No. 12 (July, 1954), pp. 13-49.

And, Paul F. Angiollilo, "Cecco Angiolieri, Scamp and Poet of Medieval Siena." Paper delivered in April 1967 at the University of Kentucky Foreign Language Conference.

[13] Alessandro D'Ancona, "Cecco Angliolieri, poeta umorista del XIII," *Nuova Antologia* (1874), XXV, pp. 5-57.

[14] Cecco Angiolieri, *Sonetti,* per cura di Aldo F. Massera (Bologna, 1906).

later, in 1934, the studiously careful research of Todaro [15] cast more than reasonable doubt on the authenticity of quite a number. Miss Todaro questioned particularly the sonnets in which the names of Meo, Mino Zeppi and Ciampolin appear, as well as the *tenzoni* which presumably represent sonnets between Cecco and others. Which are Cecco's and which those of his partner in dialogue is not always clear. Her conclusion is that about 70 sonnets are indisputably his, while the remaining 80 are open to doubt. Despite persuasive arguments, Miss Todaro herself indulges in certain assumptions where another might not. Nonetheless, her work sufficiently impressed subsequent scholars that recent editions are at pains to indicate the sonnets of dubious attribution.

Mario Marti took up the troublesome question again in 1950, noting that Todaro's work, provocative as it was, had evoked little comment.[16] Of particular interest, however, was his examination of a previously overlooked *Codex* of early poems, namely the *Escurialense e. III 23*. Therein are listed 24 sonnets attributed to Cecco, 14 of which are in the *Chigiano* but the remaining 10 in no other collection. The *Codex* contains also poems ascribed to Meo dei Tolomei, which are confusingly similar to Cecco's. Marti's article brings clarification to the subject, but he too, after extensive research prudently poses some questions.

The bulk of modern criticism, interestingly enough, hews to a Tainian approach. How better to deal with Cecco if not in terms of *race, milieu,* and *moment,* and especially *faculté maitresse?* It is upon this latter consideration that much discussion has centered. What, indeed, is his ineluctable bent, his unique cachet? Cecco is so much a product of his time and environment that any intelligent reading of his poetry must be premised upon some familiarity with the Siena of the late 13th century. Nannetti's *Cecco Angiolieri, la sua patria, i suoi tempi e la sua poesia,*[17] in particular, makes a useful contribution to this area, though much illuminating material is encountered in Ancona, Russo and others.

---

[15] Adele Todaro, *Sull'Autenticità dei Sonetti Attribuiti a Cecco Angiolieri* (Palermo, 1934).

[16] Mario Marti, "Per una Nuova Edizione dei Sonetti de Cecco Angiolieri," *Convivium*, III (1950), pp. 441-450.

[17] Elvira Nannetti, *Cecco Angiolieri, la sua patria, i suoi tempi e la sua poesia* (Siena, 1929).

INTRODUCTION   17

In the absence of further factual data, one turns naturally to the sonnets, which, if scarcely a journal of the soul, do at least offer abundant personal detail. Rarely has a poet so exteriorized his feelings. His hatreds, his loves, his irritations, his vices are all laid bare with no trace of reticence or shame. Yet never were biographical riches no fraught with peril for the critic. Precisely how to interpret the hundred-odd posturings and self divestments that Angiolieri has left remains a problem of magnitude. If his themes are paltry — and they are essentially his reactions to the daily problems that assail him — his style is often scintillating. There are fine burst of verbiage; hyperbole is played to the limit. The voluble Sienese is racy, coarse, slanderous, comic, and, an incurable and indefatigable exhibitionist. Between this frequently brilliant verbal dexterity, however, and the emotions expressed, critical interpretation has wavered, being divided essentially into two camps, as Bruno Maier has noted in his *La Personalità e la poesia di Cecco Angiolieri*. Those of romantic or positivist persuasion, including Ancona, Momigliano, Papini, Pirandello and Steiner have tended to take Cecco pretty much at face value. For them he is *l'enfant du siècle,* the *poète maudit.* For them his sufferings and celebrated "melancholy" have a Byronic verisimilitude. Subsequent critics, numbering such eminents as Russo and Sapegno, and, indeed, most of the recent commentators have stressed rather the stylistic and textual aspects of the poems, reminding us that he is a garrulous showman, a mountebank who was fully aware of his talents as an entertainer, and only too willing to pipe the tune that pleased. Maier himself resumes quite justly the crux of the matter in averring that "il problema della sincerità di Cecco e di somma importanza" and that, "se i romantici avevano visto in Cecco fuoco e crisi di coscienza, i moderni vi trovarono freddezza e cerebralità" and that neither comes to grips with what he terms "l'umanità di Cecco."[18] Interpretation of such "umanità" resides essentially in the eye and ear of the latter-day reader.

Even from a cursory reading of selected sonnets, one senses Cecco's perpetual need to verbalize. There is never the thought

---

[18] "The problem of Cecco's sincerity is of capital importance... if the Romantics have seen fire and *crises de conscience* in Cecco, the moderns find coldness and intellectualism." Bruno Maier, *La personalità e la poesia di Cecco Angiolieri* (Bologna, 1947), pp. 15-16. See also E. Rho, "Umanità di Angiolieri," *Primitivi e Romantici* (Firenze, 1937).

"that lies too deep for tears," never that inherent repugnance to reveal that which is most personal and intimate. On the contrary, he casually puts to verse sentiments that another would consider demeaning; and everywhere the showman is so evident as to put a thoughtful reader on his guard. Despite this, he has unquestionably been overinterpreted, as it were, and too many pronouncements taken literally. As Li Gotti observes: "A Cecco è capitato il caso specioso di rimanere vittima della propria calunnia." [19]

Yet unconsciously, he reveals much more than could ever have been his intent, not in statements, but rather in the atmosphere which he creates. Beyond the words one senses a troubled soul, bitter frustration, the shallowness of carping, petty ways. One seeks almost in vain for a fleeting moment of disinterestedness, of nobility or kindness. And to confuse the picture, there is ever present an artist of refreshing and distinct originality. Thus the tantalizing problem remains. What is jest, and what is truth? As with so many a Pirandellian enigma, it is one's own interpretation which must ultimately prevail.

Too often it is a temptation to seize upon a telling line or phrase to cite as characteristic of a writer's philosophy and upon which one may, with impunity, generalize. In the case of some, this assumption may be perfectly legitimate because there is an inner consistency to their work. With Angiolieri such statements lead to completely false conclusions. He must be read *in extenso*, and the single line, or sonnet, assessed within the context of his highly colored language and the temper of his times. How absurd, for example, to take "s'i' fossi foco io arderei 'l mondo" in anything approaching a literal sense. It is pure humbug, a bravura piece played to the gallery. His celebrated melancholy to which he more than once alludes: "e la mia bàlia fu malinconia," should in no sense be construed as romantic melancholy as modern criticism has been at pains to point out. With him the term connotes rather, displeasure, vexation, frustration because of unfulfilled desires. Cecco indubitably has his "ulcerated soul" as Bartoli calls it,[20] his pangs of conscience, his private anguish when the awful truth of his

---

[19] "It is the curious fortune of Cecco that he has become the victim of his own calumny" Ettore Li Gotti, *Saggi* (Firenze, 1941), p. 21.

[20] Adolfo Bartoli, *Storia della Letteratura Italiana* (Firenze, 1879), II, p. 273.

wasted years assailed him. But he enjoyed abundant resources of resilience. There was always another tavern, another woman, and surely a public ready to laugh and applaud another sonnet. So many pages have been devoted to his re-creation, yet he nimbly eludes the most learned and insistent pursuers. What is the *sincerità* of Cecco? What is his *umanità?*

The question will never be satisfactorily resolved. More than seven hundred years have elapsed since his birth. His language, like Shakespeare's may still be read almost at first glance with superficial understanding, but the original flavor, the allusions, the gay play with words, the subtle implications are, alas, in large measure irretrievably lost. Occasionally the fruits of meticulous scholarship clarify a name, elucidate a passage, or reveal an unsuspected meaning of a word, but the spontaneous, pristine quality can never be entirely recaptured. His Siena remains essentially a shadowy city. Of his personal life, we possess really little more than a handful of sterile facts. Maier very aptly likens Cecco to a canvas of Caravaggio with its mysterious chiaroscuro which intrigues and tantalizes the observer.[21]

We are drawn back ineluctably to the masterly essay of Ancona, which first focused modern attention upon the poet. Though details may have been in error, and its interpretation too patently romantic, its intuitive grasp of the subject seems largely accurate. Admitted the showmanship, the superficialities and exaggerations of Cecco, he remains a disordered personality with schizophrenic tendencies and a perenially adolescent approach to life. His sufferings surely are never of epic proportions. But to the thoughtful reader, there *is* laughter through tears and there are moments of deep unhappiness which the hyperbolic plaints and the raucous gaiety tend to obscure. Above all there is a true artist, bold and original, a technician very sure of his effects, and a poet in whom the divine afflatus occasionally burns forth brightly. In the words of Papini, that which is best in Cecco is "l'estro del poeta," his poetic inspiration or fire.[22]

---

[21] Bruno Maier, *Op. cit.*, p. 80.
[22] Giovanni Papini, *Op. cit.*, p. 104.

Chapter I

SIENA AND ANGIOLIERI

Prosperity and relative stability in the late 13th and early 14th centuries had brought a new ease and joy in living to the Tuscan region. Art, industry and trade flourished. To be sure, the threat of war was never too distant; even dread pestilence briefly brought tragedy, but basically life had savor and promise. They were thoughtless, pleasure-seeking times given to jousting and games, feasts, excursions and entertainment. Angiolieri was born at the time that Siena's prestige had reached its apogee. This redoubtable commune was still contesting with Florence the supremacy of the whole Tuscan region. Perhaps the most conspicuous of its attributes was its boundless vitality. As far as government was concerned, a rather admirable democracy prevailed, even if a bit precarious on occasion, as strong factions were involved. It boasted a governing committee or council composed at one time of as many as 36 members, but reduced ultimately to nine, the oftmentioned *Governo di Nove*. In the mid twelve-hundreds an uneasy compromise prevailed between the nobles and the populace at large. Gradually the bourgeois gained ascendancy and as accommodations were effected, the grip of the very rich was weakened, and a viable alliance of upper-class, merchant and commoner subsisted. Nor was there ever a time, moreover, that the voice of the Church was not clearly heard. In the midst of its perpetual squabbles and skirmishes with its neighbors, Siena, *vetus civitas virginis*, as she was commonly known, founded convents, monasteries and hospitals. The strain of genuine religious fervor was never wanting.

The important banking houses of the Tolomei and Buonsignori, who were for many years bankers to the Papacy, enjoyed preeminence in the world of finance until the disastrous bankruptcy in 1292 of the Buonsignori. Though this date marked the beginning of the city's decline, the seriousness of the situation was masked by a notable upsurge in artistic production.

Architecturally Siena was imposing with its fortress-like palaces, the fine Palazzo Pubblico and the arresting, rather than beautiful, Cathedral. In painting Guido da Siena was making notable contributions and Duccio, later to be known as the father of the Sienese School, was already establishing himself. The splendid pulpit of Nicola Pisano and his son, Giovanni, which graces the Cathedral, was likewise produced during these creative years.

Few cities were more sports-minded. Jousting and tournaments of various types were tremendously popular. Even organized *pugna* or fist-fight battles engaged the hardy young. It was the *palio,* however, which enjoyed the widest renown. Originally the *palii* were horse races run seasonally in conjunction with religious festivals. In those days they passed over a difficult and lengthy course marked out through the city and beyond. Distinguished entrants from all over Italy participated. The modern *palio,* which takes place within the confines of Siena, is but a faint reminder of its sturdier ancestor. It is more pageantry and show than horsemanship.

Painful contrasts between the rich and the poor indubitably existed, but today, thanks to the delightful verses of Folgore di San Gimignano we remember in particular the life of the gilded youth of the day. His sonnets present us with a vivid fresco of the elegant pastimes of the *brigata spenderrecia,* the "spendthrift brigade" of blithe young nobles with whom he consorted. Through the seasons their carefree activities ranged from banqueting, the hunt, picnics and lovemaking to any other diversion which a well-filled purse might permit.

In the field of letters, however, Siena took definitely a second place to Florence. Its literature was essentially "bourgeois," a term which is of fairly recent application. It comprised a whole coterie of satiric, comic, burlesque and realist poets best exemplified by such names as Rustico di Filippo, Nicolo del Rosso, Cecco Nuccioli, Pietro dei Faitinelli and Meo de' Tolomei. Folgore da San Gimignano stands somewhat apart, not being precisely Sienese nor bourgeois. Its most distinguished associate, Cecco Angiolieri, likewise gains a niche of his own, thanks to his more conspicious talents.

This was essentially a middle-class phenomenon. An irrepressibly sociable and garrulous populace which reveled in banter, gossip, argument and jest thronged the public squares. From this ceaseless interchange, language found new subtleties and took on a greater flexibility as it mirrored the colorful parlance of the teeming streets; and from this fluent verbalism sprang a regional, bourgeois literature. Who were its authors? — notaries, jurists, public servants, scions of well-to-do families, all men of some learning who felt the urge to write, but in treating the multifarious aspects of middle class life about them, they adopted generally a familiar language spiced with dialect and popular jargon as it served their ends. Their tone is more often than not personal and conversational; their treatment realistic, usually tending toward parody, satire and invective. It is not autochtonous literature. This, too, is to be found but rather in the popular ballad, which, engaging as it often is, remains essentially rough, awkward and lacking in those more knowledgeable qualities of workmanship, theme and invention which true bourgeois literature possesses.

This corpus of poetry by no means sprang spontaneously into being. A closer acquaintanceship reveals its ties with earlier traditions. In matters of form and poetic device it drew inevitably, even if unconsciously, from the Provenzal School. It was even more heavily indebted to Goliardic literature, particularly in matters of theme. From this latter, in fact, it borrowed much of the conventional subject matter, the tribulations of blind fortune, a lively and constant concern for money, the joys of the tavern and the mixed blessing of woman, who along with the church comes in for a generous measure of satire. Lastly, the pervasive influence of the *dolce stil nuovo* itself inescapably touches the poets of this group even as they mock and rebel against it. It is too much a part of the contemporary culture and its practitioners too distinguished to be ignored. The originality of these so-called bourgeois writers stems from the considerable skill and freshness with which they were able to rework their literary heritage in terms more meaningful to their own society, and especially in a vernacular which was properly theirs.

Their range of subject is wide. There are numerous sonnets and tenzoni dealing with political questions. Some are disputatious and abusive, others, as with Pietro de' Faitinelli and Niccolo del

Rosso are exhortations to nobler public service. Pieraccio Tebaldi in his later years offers verse that is sober and moralizing. Folgore di San Gimigniano is remembered more for his enchanting pictures of the social life of the privileged few than for his political sonnets. Money, as previously noted, provides an insistent leit-motif. These artisans and professional folk were as keenly aware of the power of silver and gold as any of their distant Balzacian cousins. Woman, an inexhaustible theme, is to these poets never an unattainable Beatrice or Laura but an earthy creature, fickle, vain, exactly their own feminine counterpart, and often even more venal into the bargain. If their accents from time to time suggest the *dolce stil nuovo,* it is only trimming. Tebaldi speaks for them when he observes:

> Amor si non è altro, ch'un desio
> Criato sol ne la concupiscenza.[1]

Rustico di Filippo might in many respects be their Henry Miller in his penchant for the stark particulars of love. Unnatural and perverted tastes find their not infrequent celebrants. It is a world teeming with all too human passions, the din of strident voices, the stench of the unwashed. What a far cry, indeed, from the Elysian fields of Cavalcanti, Guinicelli and Dante, but it is a remarkably alive and fascinating world. One must never forget, however, that concomitantly these latter and others of their persuasion were producing verse devoted to genuinely noble and idealized sentiments. The two faces of the coin are ever visible; and ultimately universal renown will be accorded Dante and his group for their infinitely more encompassing view of Man and his destiny.

Cecco Angiolieri of the eminently personal and diverting talents is purely Sienese. It is he who is to outdistance in originality and true poetic endowment the others of this corps of literate and often gifted writers. His sonnets must have been recited in the taverns and other haunts to amused and admiring listeners. They echo the familiar idiom; they reflect contemporary fashions and events, and should, of course, be interpreted within the context of this society. Angiolieri thus enjoyed a comparatively happy and fruitful period

---

[1] "Love is nothing else than an urge created solely by concupiscence"

in the tumultuous history of this resilient and colorful city. He was never to know the plague of 1348 which carried away two-thirds of its inhabitants and signaled the end of a brilliant era. Catherine of Siena and Piccolomini were yet to appear.

The sparse biographical details which are extant concerning his life are reported quite without variance by his many commentators. These data do little more than place the poet and suggest the nonconforming pattern of his life. He was born about 1260 of a well-to-do and distinguished Sienese family. The ancestral home in Via dei Re, now Via Cecco Angiolieri, bears the inscription "hanc domum coepit aedificare Angelierus in anno domini MCCXXXIV." [2] The family, because of its financial interests, was inscribed in the Arte del Cambio, the Exchange (or Brokers) Guild. The poet's father, who had been banker to Gregory IX, was twice prior, and later one of the 36 Signori del Comune. He belonged also to the Order of the Cavalieri di Santa Maria, colloquially known as the *frati gaudenti*.[3] The professed mission of the brothers was to uphold the faith against heretics, protect women, children and the poor, and guard the Holy Church from usurpers. Membership was drawn from the affluent and noble. The order unfortunately enjoyed the reputation of being something less than Christ-like in its practices which allegedly worked more to the personal advantage of its adherents than to that of the downtrodden. Dante viewed them simply as hypocrites. Cecco's mother, Lisa Salimbeni, of a family even more prestigious than the Angiolieri, was herself a *militissa* or member of the feminine contingent of the same order.

Cecco, like his parents, was a Guelf, and in 1281 did military service with the Sienese when they laid siege to and captured the Ghibelline castle of Turri in Maremma. On two occasions at this time, he was fined for absence from camp. In 1282, he was again fined for being out after curfew. In 1288, in company with his father, he was a member of a small group sent to reinforce the Florentines against Arezzo in the Battle of Campaldino. It was presumably here that he first met Dante with whom he was to exchange some verse which eventually led to a complete rupture between the two. In 1291, he was charged with having attacked and

---

[2] "Angiolieri began the construction of this house in 1234."
[3] "the jolly friars"

wounded a certain Dino de Bernardo da Monteluco, but appears to have been absolved whilst his companion in the enterprise bore the penalty. A few years later he left Siena, probably as an exile (if we are to give credence to the allusion in sonnet LXXXIV,[4]), to betake himself to Rome where he was attached to the Sienese Cardinal Riccardo Petroni. In 1302, it is recorded that he sold a vineyard for 700 lire. His presence in Rome seems to be attested until 1303. The ensuing decade is without news of him until a document dated 25 February 1313 indicates that five of his offspring renounced their paternal legacy which was completely encumbered with debts. Their disappointment must have been compounded by the fact that they were themselves obliged to make some payments for debts which the Commune believed Cecco had contracted. His death is, therefore, assumed to have been in 1312 or early 1313. Somewhere in his career he had acquired a wife, possibly one Uguccia di Gugliemo di Cortona, and six children, Meo, Deo, Angelieri, Simone, Arbolina and Tessa. Miss Todaro, however, is of the opinion that Uguccia married a Cecco of her own home town, Cortona, and not Angiolieri.[5] So much for generally accepted facts.

A quasi-biographical addendum is provided years later by Boccaccio in the *Decamerone*. The facts for his story very likely came to his ears as part of regional lore, amplified possibly by an acquaintance with Cecco's verse. In any event, he relates in the fourth story of the ninth day the unfortunate experience of Cecco, who, having very reluctantly been subsidized by his father, is about to set out for Marca d'Ancona to obtain a post in the suite of a certain cardinal. In order to make a fitting appearance he needs a man servant. One Cecco di Forterrigo, a fellow Sienese and acquaintance, begs to accompany him in this capacity. Angiolieri at first hesitates because the other Cecco "giocava et oltre a ciò s'inebbriava alcuna volta,"[6] words which are only too applicable to Angiolieri himself. Ultimately he agrees and the two set out together. In no time Angiolieri is shamefully tricked by the other, forced to strip to his shirt, and seek shelter with relatives at Corsignano. It is of passing interest

---

[4] Sonnet LXXIV, line 2: "If I see the day that I am re-admitted in Siena"

[5] Todaro, *Op. cit.*, p. 26.

[6] "was given to gambling and even got drunk occasionally"

to note that Boccaccio refers to Angiolieri as "bello e costumato uomo era." So, at least by hearsay, the poet has come down through the years as a "good-looking and well-mannered young man," who on occasion had reservations against drinking and gambling. At the same time, in terms of rascality, one feels that either Cecco might have been the perpetrator of the trick, and, in fact that Boccaccio may have had them mixed.

Portraits of the poet seem non-existent except for one with which Papini in his *Storia della Letteratura Italiana,* prefaces his account of Angiolieri. It is a pen sketch of unattributed hand. Even if entirely from the artist's imagination, it is a happy invention. The young man's features are small and regular, the lips a little mocking and sensuous and the sharp eyes those of an experienced observer of life. There is a renard-like sleekness to the physiognomy that is at once rather attractive and repellent. It goes well with the poems.

For a romanticized account of his life, indeed, a document which bears further witness to the appeal of this engaging knave, one might turn to the poetical drama of Nino Berrini, *Il Beffardo,*[7] which, in 1922, was in its seventh edition. Sapegno rather crustily characterizes it as a *dramma brutto,* an opinion which would scarcely be shared by all. The play, much in the style of Benelli, presents Cecco upon his return home after the episode reported by Boccaccio. The mother, Min Zeppa, and father would like to despatch him forthwith upon some business mission, but Cecco, and his friend, Ciampolin, decide to remain. The home scene leaves much to be desired. The father ultimately kills Min, his wife's lover, and is himself fatally injured. Much of Cecco's verse is strewn appropriately throughout the piece, and Cecco himself emerges a somewhat more human, if still shadowy figure. Surely one may say of Berrini's re-creation that *se non è vero, è ben trovato.*

A final item of passing interest is a suggestion of Dante Gabriel Rossetti that a sonnet of Guido Cavalcanti, "Se non ti caggia la sua Santalena" which Rossetti entitles, "To a Newly Enriched Man Reminding Him of the Wants of the Poor" may well be addressed to Cecco. If so, it indicates that he enjoyed some fleeting moments of prosperity presumably thanks to the inheritance of his father. Cavalcanti in the verse refers to a Bettina, which as Rossetti points

---

[7] Nino Berrini, *Il Beffardo* (Milano, 1922).

out, is a variant of Becchina, and it is largely upon this piece of evidence that the connection with Angiolieri is made. In the absence of further data pertaining to the poet, one must of necessity turn to the sonnets for a better acquaintance, and herein lies an area of speculation and controversy.

CHAPTER II

THE SONNETS

a) THE BECCHINA CYCLE

The sonnets group themselves more or less under a few general rubrics: love, hate, poverty, and the vagaries of fortune, as well as a miscellaneous category which contains some of his most brilliant efforts from a technical point of view. It is unfortunate that a more accurate chronology cannot be established. It might illumine here and there many of the obscure aspects of the poet's checkered life. But beyond a fairly obvious development in the sonnet sequence devoted to his passion for Becchina and what appears to be a plausible ordering of those treating of money, the other pieces virtually defy any accurate classification despite the painstaking efforts of many scholars.

Love in its many facets is the principal motif of the majority of the sonnets, a good half of which treat of Cecco's infatuation for a certain Becchina, the daughter of a tanner. The recital of his torments and anguish, his triumphs and cure make for an earthly love cycle. The venal and voluptuous Becchina in her coarseness and cruelty is as far removed from the seraphic ladies of the *dolce stil nuovo* as night from day.

The earlier sonnets reflect clearly enough the pervasive influence of traditional poetizing, but even in these, the strength and originality of Cecco's talent constantly burst through. He is of a completely realistic and sensual turn-of-mind, with a talent naturally oriented towards the comic rather than the courtly. He sings of love, and deeply felt love, but his treatment, stripped of its hyperbole and colorful rhetoric, is casual, matter-of-fact, not to say naturalistic.

However, so well versed is he in the practices of the aulic school, and so easily does he adapt them to his use that the unwary reader may at times fail to divine his purpose which so often is parody.

The following well-known sonnet written during the first phase of his passion for Becchina might appear superficially akin to the "new school." Yet for all his suffering — and who can doubt that he did suffer — the note of misogyny, the bluntness of the language, and the realistic overtones bespeak a completely different approach:

> Or non è gran pistolenza la mia,
> ch'i non mi posso partir dad amare
> quella che m'odia e nïente degnare
> vuol pur vedere ond'i' passo la via?
>
> E dammi tanta pena, notte e dia,
> che de l'angoscia mi fa sì sudare,
> che m'arde l'anima, e nïente non pare;
> certo non credo ch'altro 'nferno sia.
>
> Assa' potrebb'uom dirm': —A nulla giova!
> Ch'ell'è di tale schiatta nata, 'ntendo,
> che tutte son di così mala pruova.
>
> Ma per ch'i la trasamo, pur attendo
> ch'Amor alcuna cosa la rimova:
> ch'è sì possente, che 'l può far correndo.

Oh, am I not beset with the plague's pain
Since I cannot give over loving one
Who hates me — what is worse, has such disdain
She will not even glance as I pass on?
Yes, night and day she brings me such great woe
That agony with sweat my brow's besprent.
My soul burns, yet she does not care, I know.
I cannot think that Hell is different.
Often my friends say: "Is she worth your grief?
She is a woman, that you realize,
And they are all the same, and that is ill."
Yet since I love her beyond all belief,
I wait for Love to aid in my emprise.
All potent, he can do so if he will.

II (Chubb)

---

[1] All citations are from *Rimatori Comico-Realistici del Due e Trecento, A cura di Maurizio Vitale* (Torino, 1965). It might be noted, however, that

THE SONNETS   31

This is unrequited love, but in an entirely new idiom. At this stage it can scarcely be termed a burlesque of courtly love. In fact, with Angiolieri it rarely is. Despite his broadside sweeps at the *dolce stilnovisti*, his guttiness and extravagances, there is too often a fleeting revelation of genuine suffering, or often merely an undertone of veracity which prevents the poem from being truly a tongue-in-cheek production.

In the same early days of his courtship, he pens this altogether engaging verse. He is still in awe of his "lady." Perhaps he has importuned her unduly and she has just reacted stormily as she apparently was wont to do:

> Quando veggio Becchina corrucciata,
> se io avesse allor cuor di leone,
> sì tremarei com'un picciol garzone
> quando 'l maestro gli vuol dar palmata.
>
> L'anima mia vorrebbe esser non nata,
> nanzi ch'aver cotale afflizïone;
> e maledico el punto e la stagione
> che tanta pena mi fu destinata.
>
> Ma s'io devesse darmi a lo nemico,
> e' si convien che io pur trovi la via
> che io non temi el suo corruccio un fico.
>
> Però, s'e' non bastasse, io mi morrìa;
> ond'io non celo, anzi palese 'l dico,
> ch'io provarò tutta mia valentìa.

When I see my Becchina wroth at me,
Valiant though I am, who have a lion's heart,
I shake as does a schoolboy fearfully
Whose master canes his hand and makes it smart.
My soul cries: Would that I had not been born
Rather than suffer now this misery!"
Cursed be the hour and season that brought to me

---

the numbering of the sonnets is identical in the cheaper and probably more accessible Biblioteca Universale edition: Cecco Angiolieri, *Rime,* a cura di Gigi Cavalli, Rizzoli, 1959, up to and including Sonnet CVII. At that point Vitale counts the sonnet: "Simone a Cecco" as CVIII, whereas Cavalli gives it no number. Therefore those using the Cavalli edition should note that "Risposta di Cecco a Simone" is numbered CVIII and each succeeding sonnet is one number lower than in the Vitale edition.

The anguish and the sorrow of her scorn.
Yet somehow — though my soul the devil gain
Because I say this — I must find a way
To cry: "A fig for her. Nay, let her rave!"
If not, then may death take me. This I say,
Nor do conceal it, but I make it plain:
I must, I will then, prove that I am brave!

VIII (Chubb)

The simile of the frightened school boy comes refreshingly to temper his lament which would otherwise have seemed too gloomy. Already the smart réplique at the conclusion of the sonnet, a characteristic twist of Cecco's, reminds us with whom we are dealing.

The plaints continue, some in frank parody of the *stil nuovo*. They are variations on the same theme, often repetitious and of uneven quality but almost always there is an original and often extravagant touch. The indisputable artistry of Cecco becomes more apparent. Consider the following gem, one of his celebrated dialogues. The contrapuntal development is so perfect and the vivacious movement so sure in its unerring sense of rhythm. Yet as Cavalli observes, for all its humor there is a very human quality which pervades the composition. Cecco's devoted affection continues to suffer the caustic rebuffs of Becchina.

— Becchina mia! — Cecco, nol ti confesso.
— Ed i' son tu'. — E cotesto disdico.
— I' sarò altrui. — Non vi dò un fico.
— Torto mi fai. — E tu mi manda 'l messo.

— Sì maccherella. — Ell'avrà 'l capo fesso.
— Chi gliele fenderae? — Ciò ti dico.
— Se' così niffa? — Sì, contra 'l nimico.
— Non tocc'a me. — Anzi, pur tu se' desso.

— E tu t'ascondi. — E tu va' col malanno.
— Tu non vorresti. — Perché non vorrìa?
— Ché se' pietosa. — Non di te, uguanno!

— Se foss'un altro? — Cavere'l d'affanno.
— Mal ti conobbi! — Or non di' tu bugia.
— Non me ne poss'atar. — Abbieti 'l danno!

Becchina mine — I deny it, Cecco!
But I am yours — That I'll not allow.

I'll be another's — A fig I care.
You do me wrong — Send for a bailiff
No I'll call a bawd — Her skull will get cracked.
Who's to do it? — Never you mind.
You're so touchy — With those I dislike.
Well, that's not me — None other!
You're kidding — O go to hell!
You don't mean that — And tell me why not?
Because you're kind — Not with you this year
If I were another? — I might say yes,
I don't understand you — That's no lie.
I can't help myself — Tough luck for you! (XXII)

What a common termagant Becchina must have been for all of her appeal to the poet! It is a great pity to fault the deft repartee of the original by translation, but even in English, one is aware that neither Becchina nor Cecco is bound by much reticence as their little disputes unfold.

Like all lovers, Cecco daydreams — dreams in which he sets up a series of impossible conditions under which success might be his. It is a favorite rhetorical device which we encounter fairly frequently. If Becchina had any wit, she must have been amused and perhaps a little touched. Here is the sonnet:

Se 'l cor di Becchina fosse diamante
e tutta l'altra persona d'acciaio,
e fosse fredda, com'è di gennaio
in quella part', u' non può 'l sol levante;

ed ancor fosse nata d'un giogante,
sì com'ell'è d'un agevol coiaio;
ed i' foss'un, che toccasse 'l somaio,
non mi dovrebbe dar pene cotante.

Ma s'ell'un poco mi stess'a udita,
ed i' avesse l'ardir di parlare,
credo che fora mia speme compita:

ch'i' le dire' com'i' son su' a vita,
e altre cose, ch'or non vo' contare;
parm'esser certo ch'ella direbb' "ita."

Why if Becchina's heart were diamond
And all the rest of her were steel,
As cold to love as snows when they congeal

In lands to which the sun may not get round;
And if her father were a giant crown'd
And not a donkey born to stitching shoes;
Or I were but an ass myself; — to use
Such harshness, scarce could to her praise redound.
Yet if she'd only for a minute hear,
And I could speak if only pretty well
I'd let her know that I'm her happiness;
That I'm her life should also be made clear,
With other things that I've no need to tell;
And then I feel quite sure she'd answer, Yes.

XXVIII (Rossetti)

In the following he toys with a favorite contemporary theme, to whit, the possible death of the beloved and the unswerving constancy of the lover, though the lady is scarcely aware of his existence. As usual, past contrary-to-fact conditions abound providing a very fetching rime scheme in the original, which the English unfortunately cannot convey. The wildest hyperboles are set forth. The poet even delivers his ultimatum to God. Then, changing abruptly from the bombast, the sonnet quietly resolves itself into a minor key. Cecco has sustained his role as an entertainer and at the end allows himself a moment of wistful reflection: "If only she believed me, my songs would not have been in vain."

Se tutta l'acqu'a balsamo tornasse
e la terr'òr diventasse a carrate,
e tutte queste cose mi donasse
quel che n'avrebbe ben la podestate,

per che mia donna del mondo passasse,
e' li dicerei: — Misser, or l'abbiate!
ed anzi ch'al partito m'accordasse
sosterrei dura morte, en veritate.

Ché solamente du' o pur tre capegli
contra sua voglia non vorrei l'uscisse,
per caricar d'oro mille camegli.

Ma i' vorrei ched ella mel credesse;
ché tante maitinate e tanti svegli,
come li fo, non credo ch'e' perdesse.

If the world's waters became fragrant balm,
And the whole earth great carloads of rich gold,

And all this He would put into my palm,
The One Who in His hands all power doth hold,
If I'd agree my lady should know harm
And should depart the world, I'd tell him bold:
"Keep you these gifts. For me they hold no charm,
But if she dies, let death me too enfold."
For I — unless perchance she did consent —
Would not permit hurt to one hair of her head
For all the treasure a thousand camels could bear.
Would God she knew this, knew that I had spent
Full many an evening, many a morning on her.
It was time wasted, lost, gone, vanished.

XXIX (Chubb)

A persistent question which seems to tantalize every student of Angiolieri is that of his sincerity. When is he spoofing; when is he in earnest? Such shreds of sincere emotion as he possesses seem unquestionably to be in relation to this very flesh and blood Beatrice. One cannot deny that the showman usually dominates, yet fitfully through more than a score of the sonnets is heard the anguished voice of the lover. Frequently he masks his feelings with a smirk, a jest or an amusing turn of phrase. He would save face— disguise his pain. Yet a tortured love so infuses the Becchina cycle that one experiences some difficulty in highlighting individual passages. The emotion in all its intensity is a part of the very texture of these sonnets. Criticism has tended to dismiss too many lines as "traditional expressions of courtly poetry," or "phraseology of the aulic school," or to assume that if uttered by Cecco, the usage must be in jest. No writer is immune to the influences of his ambience and inevitably he employs the vocabulary and conventions of his time; but all too often in the context of an angiolierian sonnet even these familiar trappings have an unadulterated value. When Cecco exclaims:

> Anima mia, cuor del mi' corp', amore
> alquanto di merzé e pietà ti prenda
> di me, che vivo 'n cotanto dolore,
> che 'n ora 'n ora par che 'l cor mi fenda...

> My soul, heart of my body, love
> May a little mercy and pity touch you
> For my sake, for I live in such sorrow
> That momentarily I think my heart will break... (XXVI)

can we not take him at his word? Despite his penchant for exaggeration, can one merely pass off as conventional poetizing the lines:

> Io son sì altamente innamorato,
> a la mercé d'una donna e d'Amore,
> ch'e'non è al mondo re ne imperador,
> a cui volessi io già cambiar mio stato:

> I am so deeply enamored,
> At the mercy of a lady and of Love
> That there isn't in the world king or emperor
> With whom I'd change my state: (XXXIII)

A touching passage begins a subsequent and celebrated sonnet:

> I'ho tutte le cose ch'io non voglio,
> e non ho punto di quel che mi piace,
> poi ch'io non trovo con Becchina pace:
> la 'nd'io ne porto tutto 'l mio cordoglio...

> I have all the things I don't want
> And I don't have any that I do
> Since I don't find peace with Becky:
> That's the cause of all my woe. (XXXIV)

Had the lines been penned by another, no one would doubt their sincerity.

Becchina for all her mercenary and calculating ways is human and probably flattered by the ardent suit of this scion of a distinguished house, or perhaps simply to put an end to his tedious pleading — she relents. The long-sought victory is finally attained, and as Cecco notes in Sonnet XXXIV, they become lovers on the 20th of June 1291. He remarks that he gave her more kisses than there are stars in heaven, a male record, indeed! The event was apparently so memorable a one that he appends not only the date but the hour:

> —e fu di giugno, vinti dì a l'intrante
> anni mille dugento novantuno.

> —It was in June, the 20th day, just past midnight
> In the year one thousand two hundred and ninety-one.

THE SONNETS

Interestingly enough, Sonnet XXXV, which in the standard editions follows the kissing spree, is quite specific in pointing out that Becchina has not as yet given all. It may be that the June date did not mark her capitulation, though it is so interpreted generally; or conceivably Number XXXV was written before. In any case it is a delightful verse describing Cecco's happy moments of anticipation. His suit is advancing famously. Becchina has conceded much and the poet, fearful that greediness may spoil the game, bides his time. He shares with us his ardent courtship, relating his progress in allegorical terms reminiscent of *le Roman de la Rose,* except that here the elevated tone given way to frank parody in which the allegory is only too transparent. The result is an entertainingly erotic sonnet, yet one which manages to avoid downright vulgarity.

> Per ogne gocciola d'acqua, c'ha 'n mare,
> ha cento mili' allegrezze 'l meo core,
>
> e qualunqu'è di tutte la minore
> procura più ch'a' romani 'l Sudare;
>
> ch'i' seppi tanto tra dicere e fare,
> ched i' sali' su l'àlbor de l'Amore,
> ed a la sua mercé colsi quel fiore,
> ch'io tanto disïava d'odorare.
>
> E po' ch'i' fu' di quell'albero sceso,
> sì volsi per lo frutto risalire:
> ma non poteo, però ch'i' fu conteso.
>
> Ma gir mi vo' chel fior, ch'i' ho, a gioire,
> ch'assa' di volte 'n proverbio l'ho 'nteso,
> chi tutto vuole, nulla de' avire.

For every drop of water that's in the sea
There are a hundred thousand delights in my heart;
And even the least of these gives more joy
Than the Veronica procures for the Romans. *
For I've learned much twixt words and deeds
Since I scaled the tree of Love
To seize that flower whose
Fragrance I so longed to savor.
But once descended from that tree

---

* The veil or handkerchief with which St. Veronica wiped the face of Christ. An object of veneration and pride to the Romans.

> I would have climbed again to take the fruit
> But could not as I was restrained.
> So back I'll go to sniff the flower
> Mindful of the proverb I've oft times heard
> That he who'd take all ends the loser. (XXXV)

Whatever may have been the intervening steps, Cecco's ardent suit ultimately won fulfillment. Becchina herself may have been pleased with his prowess. At least she was soon sufficiently involved to speculate on a possible occurrence nine months from those hours of bliss:

> Cecco, l'umiltà tua m'ha si rimossa
> Che giammai ben né gioia 'l mie cor sente
> Se di te nove mesi non vo grossa
>
> Cecco your humility so convinced me—
> —For never will my heart feel joy or bliss
> Unless I've a child by you nine months hence (XXXIX)

There is no record that her wish was ever fulfilled.

Becchina dominates a score of other sonnets which reflect Cecco's varying states of mind. In the following, disposed to meet her lover halfway, she summons him to a tryst.

> La mia donna m'ha mandato un messo
> Ch'i non lasci per nulla ch'i non vada
> A lei per la più diritta strada
> Ch'i posso conservando me stesso.
>
> My lady has sent me a message
> That without delay I come to her
> By the most direct route I know
> But bids me conserve my vigor (XLII)

Apparently the fires do not burn so brightly. She is, alas, three days' ride away and Cecco has no horse. Obviously making the journey on foot, he cannot arrive "vigorous" as she would have him. He concludes with an appeal to an imaginary listener:

> Vedette s'i la posso aitare?
>
> Do you see any way I can aid her?

THE SONNETS

Another saucy dialogue, a *battibecco* as it is termed in Italian, which translates quite effectively in English as "batting their beaks together" shows the pair in another of their inevitable arguments. Presumably this time Cecco has been unfaithful. He is contrite and she is vengeful. There is a perennially human quality as one egotism meets another.

(C.) — Becchin'amor! — (B.) — Che vuo', falso tradito?
— Che mi perdoni. — Tu non ne se' degno.
— Merzé, per Deo! — Tu vien' molto gecchito.
— E verrò sempre. — Che sarammi pegno?

— La buona fé. — Tu ne se' mal fornito.
— No inver' di te. — Non calmar, ch'i' ne vegno.
— In che fallai? — Tu sa' ch'i' l'abbo udito.
— Dimmel', amor. — Va', che ti veng'un segno!

— Vuo' pur ch'i' muoia? — Anzi mi par mill'anni.
— Tu non di' ben. — Tu m'insegnerai.
— Ed i' morrò. — Omè che tu m'inganni!

— Di tel perdoni. — E che, non te ne vai?
— Or potess'io! — Tègnoti per li panni?
— Tu tieni 'l cuore. — E terrò co' tuo' guai.

Becky, love — What do you want, traitor?
That you pardon me — You're not worth it.
Mercy, for God's sake — Very downcast, aren't you?
And always will be — What guarantee have I?
My good faith! — Precious little you've got.
Lots for you — No sweet talk or I'll smash you.
How have I failed? — You know, I've heard.
Tell me, love. — Be off, drop dead!
Do you want me to die? — Have for a thousand years.
You're not nice. — I suppose you'll teach me.
I'll die. — You're kidding again.
May God forgive you. — What, not gone yet?
If only I could. — Am I holding your coat?
You hold my heart. — And shall to your sorrow.

(XLVII)

It is, as ever, fresh and sparkling this conversational form which he manages so felicitously. In his hands it has a vividly personal stamp, a pulsatingly human quality and an unexpectedness which set it quite apart from the usual *contrasto*.

Inevitably in the course of his romance, Cecco also becomes prey to jealousy. Becchina, who had an eye for any comely young man with a few *soldi* to spend unfortunately did not make for the most faithful of girl friends. When Cecco learns of her lapses he vents his rage in strong and telling invective:

> Maladetto sie l'or e 'l punt'e 'l giorno
> e la semana e 'l mese e tutto l'anno
> che la mia donna mi fece uno 'nganno,
> il qual m'ha tolt'al cuor ogni soggiorno,
>
> ed hal si 'nvolto tutto 'ntorno intorno
> d'empiezza, d'ira, di noia e d'affanno
> che per mio bene e per mi' minor danno,
> vorrei lo 'nnanzi 'n un ardente forno...
>
> Cursed be the hour, the moment, the day
> The week, the month, indeed the whole year
> In which my lady played me false
> Snatching from my heart all repose
> Twisting it round and round
> With angry passions, wrath and strife
> Till, for my good, or rather, my lesser pain
> I'd toss it in a burning furnace — ... (LI)

Rarely have the pangs of jealousy and unrequited love been more picturesquely depicted than in the heartfelt sonnet XLIX. It is a gripping piece which belongs quite rightfully among the sonnets which can be characterized beyond question as "sincere."

> Qualunque giorno non veggio 'l mi' amore,
> la notte come serpe mi travollo
> e sì mi giro, che paio un bigollo,
> tanta è la pena che sente 'l meo core.
>
> Parmi la notte ben cento mili'ore,
> dicendo: — Dio, sarà ma' dì, vedrollo?
> e tanto piango, che tutto m'immollo,
> ch'alcuna cosa m'alleggia 'l dolore.
>
> Ed i' ne son da lei così cangiato,
> che 'n una ched e' giungo 'n sua contrada,
> sì mi fa dir ch'i' vi son troppo stato

>   e ched i' voli, sì tosto men vada,
>   però ch'ell'ha 'l su' amor a tal donato,
>   che per un mille più di me li aggrada.
>
>   A day goes by and I don't see my love
>   At night, like a snake, I writhe in bed
>   And turn and twist as might a trout
>   Such is the pain that's in my heart.
>   Night seems to have a hundred thousand hours:
>   Oh Lord, will day ever dawn, will I see it?
>   So much I weep that I am wet with tears.
>   Yet nothing lightens my sorrow;
>   Indeed, this is the way that she rewards me:
>   Scarcely do I reach her town when she has
>   Someone tell me i've been there too long,
>   That as soon as I will, I'd better be off,
>   That she's fallen in love with so-and-so
>   Who pleases her a thousand times more than I. (XLIX)

Misogynous passages occur; he rails against his poverty; longs to recapture the first joys of love, reveals in a hundred ways his restless, craving soul. These conflicting emotions are in a sense summed up in LV, one of the last of this group. Herein his affair with Becchina has reached its nadir:

>   Ogn'altra carne m'è 'n odio venuta
>   e solamente d'un becco m'è 'n grado,
>   e d'essa m'è la voglia sì cresciuta,
>   che, s'i' non n'ho, che Di' ne campi! arrado.
>
>   Quella, cu' è, mi dice ch'è venduta,
>   e ch'i' son folle, ch'i' averne bado;
>   ché s'i' le dessi un marco d'or trebuta,
>   non ne potre' avere quant'un dado.
>
>   Ed i' com'uomo, cu' la fitta tocca,
>   ché so che voglion dir quelle parole,
>   sì do ad altre novelle di bocca.
>
>   E Die sa come 'l cor forte mi dole,
>   per ch'i' non ho de' fiorin a ribocca,
>   per poter far e dir ciò ch'ella vuole.
>
>   Every other flesh is repugnant to me
>   For only Becky gives me joy
>   My longing for her has so grown

> That if I can't have her, may I be damned, I rage!
> They say she sells herself for gold
> I'm mad to fight for her so much
> For if I paid her tribute with a golden mark
> I'd only get a penny's worth.
> As the man who bears the wound
> I know what these words really mean,
> So let me talk of other things.
> God alone knows how my heart aches
> Since I don't have florins in hand
> To meet her every whim.
>
> (LVI)

If the sentiments are not new, there is at least a note of veracity which is compelling. The sonnet is notably well composed with a balance and linguistic unity that are not precisely the trademark of Angiolieri. The tone is one of bitter resignation. There are few extravagances to distract. The first three lines noting simply the agonizing sexual ties which bind him to Becchina are arresting, indeed, even to the pathetic little play upon the "becco" which refers to Becchina, of course, but the word suggests as well "a taste of" "a nibble." The climax of the sonnet comes swiftly in the succeeding line with its cry of enraged despair and frustration: *arrado*. The second quatrain affords in effect a flashback. Someone has just reminded Cecco that Becchina is a whore — the unhappy fact that he has sought to forget. He recalls at the same time that his money, which we know to be in lamentably short supply, seems to be worth less than any other fellow's. The tercet which follows bespeaks, after his explosion of rage, the bitter acceptance which must be his: "Do ad altre novelle di bocca" "I'll have to talk of other things." The final tercet, however, snatches the sonnet somewhat from its black mood with a characteristically angiolierian twist. God knows how I suffer, for my pockets aren't stuffed with florins to do her bidding. He comes up fighting as it were. He has almost enough spunk left to make a jest. One is reminded of Papini's observation that young Angiolieri writes not from the heart but from the viscera and from "genitali insoddisfatti."[2] Essentially this may be true, but the heart does on occasion speak quite tellingly. Maier states the case more graciously in nothing that Cecco is of a changeable nature,

---

[2] G. Papini, *Storia della letteratura d'Italia* (Firenze, 1937), p. 19.

incapable of prolonged or stable emotions.[3] In any event he has reached his Calvary. The worst is now over, a fact which he avers quite laconically:

> Ella disamorò ed io ancora
>
> She fell out of love and I too (LVII)

The withdrawal symptoms are a little painful. He rails, complains and philosophizes, but the sting is gone. He can now observe with reflective candor:

> Io combattei con Amor ed hol morto
> e ch'i' ho tanto pugnato mi pento;
>
> I fought with Love and killed him
> And am annoyed I was so long doing it; (LX)

and further:

> I' sono innamorato, ma non tanto
> che non men passi ben leggeramente:
> ... ...
> che troppo amare fa gli omini stolti ...
>
> I'm in love, but not so much
> That I can't do without it nicely
> ... ...
> Anyway, too much loving makes men stupid ... (LXII)

He alludes to other amours (e.g. LXIII) but ultimately the cycle on love terminates with a cynical bit (LXIV) in which he maintains that he who is in love might as well recognize that very likely his mother cursed him before he was born — perhaps before he was conceived — for he will know no peace; but the crowning blow he has ever suffered — and Cecco draws on his personal experience — is to have the beloved die a virgin. Cecco's sentimental journey has not been particularly elevating. Love in its most mundane and degrading aspects has paraded before us, permitting us to witness the intensely human, the comic, the terrible — the reverse of the

---

[3] B. Maier, *La personalità e la poesia de Cecco Angiolieri* (Bologna, 1947), p. 142.

medal, as it were — not an entirely agreeable experience perhaps, but surely a most illuminating one. Whether Cecco himself, utterly disenchanted, went on to explore the unorthodox, we cannot be sure. Such a possibility is envisaged, however, in the discussion on the sonnets of dubious attribution.

b) MONEY THEMES AND FAMILY

It is scarcely surprising that some fifteen of the hundred odd sonnets should turn on the theme of money — or more precisely, the lack of it. Cecco indubitably gave evidence early in life of a complete incompetence in money matters. His affluent parents obviously were not disposed to entrust their stingily administered funds to his loose-handed dealing. Unattractive as they may have been, one can appreciate their decision since Cecco never could find a gainful way of life, and left, as we are aware, an estate so encumbered with debts that his offspring were obliged to renounce it. Yet this very shortcoming is turned to literary profit for the poet could treat his indigence with wry humor. As a theme it is remarkably fruitful and the inspiration of some of his most telling lines.

The money cycle, if it may be so termed, has been very intelligently arranged. One has no idea of when or in what order were written the sonnets which fall under this heading, but as presented in the standard editions, they show an interesting themal development which seems completely plausible. In medieval literature, speculation on the vagaries of fortune provided a fecund source for the poet. We find lyrics in praise of money, lamentations over its lack, as well as the most varied reflections on the operations of Dame Fortune's wheel. Apart from his own lively, personal interest in the matter, Cecco was, at the same time, simply making use of a popular topic. The first of this series begins auspiciously enough in praise of money with the poet expressing himself in his usual forthright fashion:

> In questo mondo, chi non ha moneta
> per forza è necessario che si ficchi
> uno spiedo per lo corpo o che s'impicchi...

> In this world he who has no money
> Obviously might as well run a spear
> Through himself, or put a noose 'round his neck...
>
> (LXVI)

Though he disclaims personal experience, the poet notes that the man who has money is usually at pains to make more. And should one venture to ask why, Cecco expostulates enthusiastically, "argento, che fa l'uom poeta." "Why money makes man a veritable poet, what's more, cures the sick, creates landholders and even civilizes a churl. If I'm kidding," he concludes, "May God strike me dead!"

A colorful variant is LXVII which dwells rather upon the lot of the poor man to whom:

> E dolci pomi li paion amari...
>
> Even sweet apples seem sour to him... (LXVII)

It begins with the trenchant simile of the pauper who resembles a picked bird:

> Così è l'uomo che non ha denari,
> Com'è l'uccel quand è vivo pelato;
> Li uomin di salutarlo son cari:
> com'un malato sel veggion da lato.
>
> A penniless man
> Is like a bird skinned alive;
> People are chary of greeting him,
> Indeed they shun him like a leper... (LXVII)

But this time another remedy is suggested. Let him drown himself — and today rather than tomorrow — so that death, not life, can attend to him. The verse ends, however, on a brighter note, though Cecco's philosophy could not be more materialistic. The chap who has a well-filled purse finds that men say of him, "You're better than the staff of life! And what he wants he gets with no more effort than he'd take to twirl a stick."

As the money theme develops one finds, of course, reflections of the poet's personal involvements. He concludes that there is no success in love without money. Whether your tastes be high or low, money is the key. Sonnet LXIX reminds us that Becchina's love fluctuated with the florin, and of the low esteem in which she held him when money was short:

> Or udite, signor, s'i'ho ragione
> ben di dovermi impiccar per la gola:
> poi che la povertà mi ten a scola,
> madonna m'ha più a vile ch'un moscione...
>
> Just tell me, friend, if I'm not right
> To feel that I must slit my throat;
> Since I've become poverty's apprentice
> My lady considers me less than a fruit fly... (LXIX)

Cecco possesses something of the same keen sense of observation of nature that La Fontaine will display so abundantly some centuries later. How to reduce man to more complete insignificance than to liken him to a fruit fly? In a succeeding sonnet, the picture of the bear licking its paws from hunger summons to the imagination all of the ingratiating world of *Le Roman de Renart*:

> Un denaio, non che far cottardita
> avessi sol, tristo! ne la mia borsa!
> ch'e mi conven far di quelle de l'orsa
> che per la fame si lecca le dita;
>
> Had I, poor wretch, but a farthing in my purse
> —I've not even enough to buy a skirt
> (Becchina may well have asked for one)
> Now all I can do is to imitate the bear
> Who licks his paws from hunger pangs. (LXX)

Life appears so depressing that he concludes that he might as well buy a cord and hang himself on the street corner. But then, tongue-in-cheek, he observes that only horror of "the great sin," to whit, suicide, restrains him. The hyperbolic threat of self-destruction, which strikes us today as both macabre and tiresome, was probably for his listeners merely part and parcel of his habitually extravagant language. Cecco is the perfect cafe artist, the incomparable diseur. Sonnet LXXI affords an entirely representative example of his technique, his fondness for the "gag," his chimerical comparisons and far-flung emotional debauches.

> Di tutte cose mi sento fornito,
> se non d'alquante ch'i' non metto cura,

come di calzamento e d'armadura;
di ben vestire i' son tutto pulito,

e co' danari son sì mal nodrito,
più ch'i' del diavol, di me han paura;
altri diletti, per mala ventura,
più ne son fuor, che gennaio del fiorito.

Ma sapete di che i' ho abbondanza?
Di ma' desnar con le cene peggiori,
e male letta, per compier la danza.

Gli altri disagi non conto, signori,
ché troppo sarebbe lunga la stanza:
questi so nulla, appo gli altri maggiori.

With everything I feel I'm quite well provided,
Except for such items as I don't really care about —
Let's say footgear and armor;
Of proper clothing I'm quite destitute,
And as for money, am I ill-heeled!
It fears me more than I the devil.
Of other amenities, unfortunately
I'm as bare as January is of flowers.
But do you know what I have in abundance?
Poor dinners and worse suppers;
A sad sack for making love.
The other inconveniences don't count, my friends
It would take too long to relate them
And these are nothing compared to the rest. (LXXI)

One can almost hear his recital, the tone of mock modesty, the comic exaggerations, the pause for a laugh, his subtle play to the audience, all accompanied no doubt with eloquent gesture, the casual conversational tone with allusions to aspects of his life with which his acquaintances were surely familiar. It is a stylish little scenario, tailor-made for the tavern crowd. Sonnet LXXIII likewise merits attention on several counts. It begins the celebrated lines which Cecco's contemporary, Meo dei Tolomei was to appropriate subsequently for his own use. It contains also a reference to the small unproductive farm which appears to have been one of the last remains of the Angiolieri patrimony, an interesting note valuable as a biographical detail where so few exist. Again he voices his plaint against the costly infatuation which obsesses him and concludes with a shameless admission of his incurably spendthrift ways:

I' son sì magro, che quasi traluco,
de la persona no, ma de l'avere;
ed abbo tanto più a dar, che avere,
che m'è rimaso vie men d'un fistuco.

Ed èmmi sì turato ogni mi' buco,
ch'i' ho po' che dar e vie men che tenere:
ben m'è ancora rimas'un podere
che frutta l'anno il valer d'un sambuco!

Ma non ci ha forza, ch'i so 'nnamorato:
ché s'i' avesse più or che non sale,
per me sarìa 'n poco temp'assommato.

Or mi paresse almeno pur far male!
Ma con più struggo, più ,son avvïato
di voler far di nuovo capitale.

I am so thin that light well nigh shines through me —
I do not mean of person but of purse —
And owe such a lot more than any owe me,
There's not a straw left that I could disburse.
My income's gone to wrack. To my great harm,
I've naught to give away and less to keep.
True, I still have and hold my little farm.
Its fruit each year's so small I'd sell it cheap.
But 't is my fate, who bound am by love's thong,
And if I'd the world's gold, it would be still,
To spend and to go bankrupt in a day.
Would God I had the sense to not do wrong!
No use, instead I strive and always will
To get my hands on more to throw away.

LXXIII (Chubb)

Whatever one may think of the scoundrel, one cannot but admire him for his candor. Yet it is disarming, this apparent frankness with which he offers his confidences. His quixotic talent is such that he can elicit sincere sympathy for what is indubitably his very real distress, but a moment later he delivers a rapier thrust of wit, he mocks, or simply gives forth with a broadside of vulgarity; and the reader — or better, his audience — taken aback, gasps, then laughs at his sudden turn, yet sometimes remains emotionally at a loss. Cecco is a consumate showman. His "act," and this is exactly what it was, is superbly timed. Almost without exception he has an arresting first line. The center section occasionally faults through abrupt transitions, or filler material, but invariably the conclusion throws its punch. The *scenari* are vigorous and pungent. He plays with his auditors as skillfully as any latter-day diseur, exciting, lulling, shocking them as suits his fancy. What a pity never to have heard his recitations!

Note the originality of the imagery in the following lines from LXXV. In hard times when he can lay his hands on very few *soldi,* he remarks:

>—Son come vin che è du'part acqua, leno,
>E son più vil, che non fu pro' Tristano;
>e 'nfra le genti vo col capo 'n seno
>più vergognoso ch'un can foretano;

>I'm like wine that's two parts water — weak,
>And am more vile than Tristan was courageous;
>I walk among the crowd with head hung low,
>More shameful than a common cur. (LXXV)

This effective beginning has a pathos which disposes the reader at once in Cecco's favor. Then within the confines of the stringently limited sonnet form he does an abrupt about-turn to comment laconically that, should anyone succeed in relieving him of the little he has — well, it's practically gone in any case, because — and here the mood suddenly changes as he concludes in tones of mock piety which deceive no one:

>che non mi piace 'l prestar ad usura
>a mo' de' preti e de' ghiotton frati.

>For I don't like lending money at usury
>The way priests and gluttonous friars do. (LXXV)

LXXVII in its exordium resembles other sonnets on the same thesis, namely "better to be dead than poor" and "when my pockets are full I've the courage of a lion." In its final sextet, however, he is apparently in a more prudent frame of mind, and one might hope for better things:

>Ma s'i' veggio mai 'l dì ch'i ne raggiunga
>ben lo terrò più savio che Merlino,
>a ch'i dena' mi trarrà de la punga,
>E di gavazze parrò fiorentino,—

>For if I ever see the day that I have any (money)
>I'll consider anyone who can draw it from my fist

> Wiser than Merlin, and as for squandering it
> You'd think I was a Florentine — (considered tight-fisted
>   by the Sienese) (LXXVII)

Such a resolve is scarcely in character, of course, and moments later he exclaims:

> I nessun modo mi poss'acconciare
> ad aver voglia di far massarizia:
> ... ...
> Assa' portrebb'om dar del cap'al muro
> ma se non ven de la propria natura
> niente vale: 'n mia fede 'l vi giuro.
>
> In no wise can I resign myself
> to be willing to economize
> ... ...
> As well might a man butt his head against the wall;
> If (thrift) doesn't come naturally
> Nothing avails: upon my word, I swear it. (LXXVIII)

A more picturesque sonnet in the same vein and otherwise interesting in its allusion to a new character, namely his wife, is LXXIX:

> Per ogni oncia di carne che ho addosso,
> e' ho ben cento libre di tristizia,
> né non so che si sia a dir letizia:
> così mia donna mi tene ad escosso.
>
> Pare ch'ella mi franga d'osso in osso,
> quando mi dice: — Fa' ben massarizia,
> e po' ti darò denari a divizia —,
> anzi vorrei esser gittat'a un fosso.
>
> E' non m'è viso che sia altro inferno,
> se non la massarizia maledetta;
> e più mi spiace, che 'l piover d'inverno.
>
> Ma quale è vita santa e benedetta,
> secondo i gran medici di Salerno?
> S'tu voi star san, fa' ciò che ti diletta.
>
> For every ounce of flesh my ribs support,
> I wear a hundred pounds of misery,
> Nor do I even know what joy may be.
> My lady, you see, keeps me on rations short.

She makes me skin and bones with her tongue's sport.
She hags; "Be close. Practice economy.
Then only will I give you of coin a mort."
There's nothing that is blacker or more hell
Than this damned penny-pinching, that I swear.
I hate it worse than freezing winter rain.
How should we really live, if we'd live well?
Hear what the doctors of Salerno declare:
Do what delights you, then you'll ne'er feel pain.

LXXIX (Chubb)

This passing reference to domestic tension serves to remind us that Cecco had a wife. The following sonnet (LXXX) affords her a more formal presentation whilst re-echoing familiar lamentations. It is of good construction, rich in original imagery and makes its appearance in anthologies as an entirely typical production:

La stremità mi richer per figliuolo,
ed i' l'appello ben per madre mia;
e 'ngenerto fu' dal fitto duolo,
e la mia bàlia fu malinconia,

e le mie fasce si fur d'un lenzuolo,
che volgarment'ha nome riccadìa;
da la cima del capo 'nfin al suolo
cosa non regna 'n me che bona sia.

Po' quand'i' cresciuto, mi fu dato
per mia ristorazion moglie che garre
da anzi dì 'nfin al ciel stellato;

e 'l su' garrir paion mille chitarre:
a cu' la moglie muor, ben è lavato
se la ripiglia, più che non è 'l Farre.

Dire want claims me as her son
And I am wont to call her mother.
My sire was deep gloom;
My nurse was melancholy.
My swaddling clothes of that cloth
That's known as tedium.
From the top of my head to the soles of my feet
There's not a single thing that's right.
Once grown they gave me for my consolation
A wife who shrills from break of day to starry night

With a chatter that is like a thousand guitars.
He who loses his wife is an idiot
To take another unless she's a good lay. (LXXX)

The wife merges from these two sonnets albeit a little sketchily but with a strong element of plausibility. Is she not, in fact, just the person the parents might have selected for their son's "ristorazion," older, pennywise, full of prudent advice, rendered more shrill and complaining as children arrived to add to her responsibilities of caring for this greatest child of all. In any case, we learn little more of her unless she served as the model for the thoroughly entertaining sonnet CXIV. It is among the pieces considered of dubious attribution by Cavalli and dismissed by Todaro as being of unknown authorship. One cannot be sure; but it is not beyond the realm of possibility that the wife may have inspired the unflattering first section:

Quando mie donn'esce la man del letto
che non s'ha post'ancor del fattibello,
non ha nel mondo sì laido vasello,
che, lungo lei, non paresse un diletto;

così ha 'l viso di bellezze netto
fin ch'ella non cerne col burattello
biacca, allume scagliuol'e bambagello:
par a veder un segno maladetto!

Ma rifassi d'un líscio smisurato,
che non è om che la veggia 'n chell'ora,
ch'ella nol faccia di sé 'nnamorato.

E me ha ella così corredato,
che di null'altra cosa metto cura,
se non di lei: o ecc'om ben ammendato.

In the morning when my lady slips from bed
Before she's had a chance to put her make-up on,
There's no mug in all the world so ugly
That next to hers would not be sheer delight.
Until she's worked with unguents, creams and paint
A semblance of good looks to simulate,
You'd think you saw a cursed witch.
But once done up with her astounding skill,
There's not a man who views her then

> Whom she does not infatuate;
> And she has so taken me in
> That I care about naught else; you might say
> There's a guy whose got it made. (CXIV)

The piece is Angiolierian in its pleasure in hyperbole as my lady metamorphoses herself from the ugliest thing in creation to one of the most irresistable. The very texture of the verse suggests Cecco. Yet there is a dichotomy which eludes satisfactory explanation. In her unmade-up state she might well be the poet's wife. The ungracious remarks are those of a disenchanted husband who wakes to view a spectre at his side, done up in crimpers, devoid of color, eyelashes and whatever. In this respect she takes her place easily in the family portrait gallery. But the gallant second half of the sonnet and the atmosphere of connubial bliss which it radiates tend to favor Miss Todaro's theory that the lady is mistress rather than wife. Or both the ladies may be involved. Alas it is another aspect of the rogue's career which we may never satisfactorily fathom.

His diatribes against poverty focus ultimately upon his father whose niggardliness he judges to be the cause of most of his ills. The theme of indigence is, in effect, terminated at this juncture, as thoroughgoing hatred of his sire takes over as a dominating phobia. Probably never in the history of letters has a father been so excoriated. A good share of Cecco's notoriety stems from this theme which has shocked many generations of readers. While many an outrageous passage may be chalked up to extravagant jest and drunken bravado as he is egged on by an amused public, the references to his parents — in particular to his father — are characterized by a venom which cannot be gainsaid. However justified his rancor may have been and however fiercely amusing the sonnets may on occasion be, they cannot but bespeak a singularly warped mind.

The frequent and exacerbated references to the father point to a difficult and unlovable individual. To the son, his dour ways, his bland hypocrisy, stinginess and longevity spelled anathema. An introduction to pater occurs in a wholesale complaint which he launches against father, mother, Becchina and Love.

> Babb'e Becchin, l'Amor e mie madre
> m'hanno sì come tord'a siepe stretto;
> prima vo'dir quel che mi fa mi'padre
> che ciascun dì da lu' son maladetto...

> The old man, Becchina, Love and my mother
> have trapped me like thrush in a hedge;
> First let me tell you what my father does:
> There's not a day that I'm not cursed by him...
>
> (LXXXV)

In the celebrated *S'io fosse foco, arderei il mondo,* Cecco in his self-devised holocaust observes quite forthrightly:

> S'i fosse morte andarei da mio padre
> s'i fosse vita fuggirei da lui
>
> If I were death I should go to my father
> If I were life I'd flee from him (LXXXVI)

In other words father is to be doomed to annihilation whatever force may be in power. In LXXXVIII, after suggesting suicide for penniless lovers, the poet notes that should one wonder why he doesn't take his own advice, it is simply that:

> c'ho un mi' padre vecchissimo e ricco,
> ch'aspetto ched e' muoi a mano a mano
> ed e' morrà quando 'l mar sarà sicco,
> si l'ha Dio fatto, per mio strazio, sano.
>
> Because my father is very old and rich
> And I expect eventually he'll die
> And die he will, but when the sea is dried up
> Since God, for my mortification, has made him tough.

A splendid sonnet in this same category, admirable for its literary effects and rather dreadful in its attitude toward the father, is XC. Again, he utilizes a series of impossible conditions which might come to pass before old Angiolieri would ever give up the ghost:

> I' potre' anzi ritornare in ieri
> e venir ne la grazia di Becchina,
> o 'l diamante tritar come farina,
> o veder far misera vit'a frieri,
>
> o far la pancia di messer Min Pieri,
> o star content'ad un piè di gallina,
> ched e' morisse ma' de la contina
> que' ch'è domonio e chiamas'Angiolieri.

Però che Galïeno ed Ipocràto,
fossono vivi, ognun di lor saprebbe,
a rispetto di lu', men che 'l Donato.

Dunque, quest'uom come morir potrebbe,
che sa cotando ed è sì naturato,
che, come struzzo, 'l ferr'ismaltirebbe?

I could sooner return to yesterday
And be in favor with Becchina,
Or grind diamonds as one would flour,
Or see the happy friars do without,
Or grow a paunch like Min Pieri,
Or be content to dine on chicken feet,
Before that demon called Angiolieri,
Would ever die of the fever.
Even if Galen and Hippocrates were living
They'd know less with respect to him
Than might some mere grammarian,
For how could this man die
Whom nature has constructed so
That, like the ostrich, he can digest iron. (XC)

The father's elephant hide, incomparable digestion and unshakeable health, in fact, receive frequent comment. Another sonnet (LXXXIX) expatiates in no uncertain terms upon the theme... Cecco avers in but slightly paraphrased terms "If I thought that I'd live one more day than that fellow who makes my life so wretched I'd thank Christ many times, but before that will ever happen, the pier at Genoa will cave in. The old critter is so stuffed with ill-gained goods that death can't enter him at either end. If you think I haven't reason for my rancor, just hear this. The other day the doctor told me that nothing but old age could kill him off. Certainly filial instincts are at low ebb. Other verses in much the same vein follow. In one amusing piece, Cecco, in propitiary tones of mock solemnity calls upon death to act impartially and with all haste in a matter of grave concern:

O che t'uccidi me o lo 'ncoiato

Either kill me or him whose hide is tough as leather

(XCII)

"Regardless of which of us you take," concludes the poet, "I'll be the winner." One can surmise the tenor of domestic life in the Angiolieri household from the following. A small incident, so homely as to be uninvented, unleashes the pent-up rancor of Cecco in a torrent of abuse:

> Il pessimo e 'l crudele odio, ch'i' porto
> a diritta ragione al padre meo,
> il farà vìvar più, che Botadeo.
> e di ciò, buon dì, me ne sono accorto.
>
> Odi, Natura, se tu ha' gran torto:
> l'altrier li chiesi un fiasco di raspeo,
> che n'ha ben cento cogna 'l can giudeo,
> in verità, vicin m'ebbe che morto.
>
> —S'i' gli avessi chèsto di vernaccia! —
> diss'io, solamente a lui approvare:
> sì mi volle sputar entro la faccia.
>
> E poi m'è detto ch'i nol debbo odiare!
> Ma chi sapesse ben ogni sua taccia
> direbbe: — Vivo il dovresti mangiare!
>
> The limitless and cruel hatred that I bear
> My father — and with right good reason
> Will make him live longer than the Wandering Jew;
> Of that, for long, I've been aware.
> Hear, O Nature, how you've wronged me.
> The other day I asked for a flask of common wine
> Of which the old Jewish dog has many hundreds.
> In truth, he all but killed me.
> "Suppose I'd asked for nectar," said I,
> Only to put him to a test.
> He all but spit in my face.
> And still I'm told I musn't hate him?
> Well if you knew better all his faults
> You'd answer, "You really ought to chew him up alive."
>
> (XCIV)

The leitmotif for the father is one of black humor, if indeed there be any element of humor in it. Ultimately time prevails and old Angiolieri passes to his reward. The occasion is celebrated with what is probably a unique eulogy in the annals of literature. Cecco is jubilant; the sonnet a paen of joy:

Non si disperin quelli de lo 'nferno,
po' che n'è uscito un che v'era chiavato,
el quale è Cecco, ch'è così chiamato,
che vi credea stare in sempiterno.

Ma in tale guisa è rivolto il quaderno,
che sempre viverò glorificato
po' che messer Angiolieri è scoiato,
che m'affliggea di state e di verno.

Muovi, nuovo sonetto, e vanne a Cecco,
a quel che giù dimora a la Badia:
digli che Fortarrigo è mezzo secco,

che non si dia nulla maninconia,
ma di tal cibo imbecchi lo suo becco,
ch'e' viverà più, ch'Enoch ed Elia.

Oh, let you not despair who live in Hell
For here is one who's 'scaped its lock and key,
And that is Cecco as you know full well
Who thought he'd dwell there through eternity.
But now the page is turned and in such wise
That from henceforth I'll only know great joy.
My father's left his hide — Angiolieri dies
At last, who all year long brought such annoy.
O sonnet, to that other Cecco go
Who, in the monastery, does nothing but brood.
And say his sire, Fortarrigo, too is half dead,
Wherefore he should abjure all thought of woe
And cram his craw with this immortal food,
And longer live than Enoch and. Elijah did.

(XCVI (Chubb)

As if this incontinent joy were not enough, Cecco cannot resist a post scriptum, as it were (XCVII), couched in tones of mock repentance. It represents, as Cavalli notes, the very height of cynicism:

Chi dice del suo padre altro, ch'onore,
la lingua gli dovrebbe esser tagliata;
per che son sette le mortal peccata,
ma enfra l'altre quell'è lo maggiore.

S'eo fosse priete o ver frate minore,
al papa fora la mia prima andata;

e direi: — Padre Santo, una crociata
si faccia indosso a chi lor fa disnore.

E s'alcun fosse, per lo su' peccato,
che 'n quel stallo ci veniss'a le mani,
vorrei che fosse cotto e poi mangiato

dagli uomini no, ma da' lupi e cani.
Dio mel perdoni, ch'io n'ho già usato
motti non bei, ma rustichi e villani.

Who utters of his father aught but praise,
'Twere well to cut his tongue out of his mouth;
Because the Deadly Sins are seven, yet doth
No one provoke such ire as this must raise.
Were I a priest, or monk in anyways,
Unto the Pope my first respects were paid,
Saying, "Holy Father, let a just crusade
Scourge each man who his sire's good name gainsays."
And if by chance a handful of such rogues
At any time should come into our clutch,
I'd have them cooked and eaten then and there,
If not by men, at least by wolves and dogs.
The Lord forgive me! for I fear me much
Some words of mine were rather foul than fair.

XCVII (Ruskin)

And, to be sure, Cecco had said many more disobliging things against his father than space permits reporting. One wonders if with all his penchant for reciting he had ventured to give public utterance to some of the more outrageous. Even the denizens of the low taverns which gave him enthusiastic hearing would surely have been put off by so crude a display of poor taste. Perhaps these verses were simply scribbled to give vent to his dismal humor for the sentiments are often times so dire and unnatural that they could not have elicited a very warm response. One can only hope so.

In the literary memorial of their offspring, Cecco's mother fares little better than her spouse. The more spectacular poems once thought to have been directed against her have, in recent years, been ascribed with fair certainty to Meo de' Tolomei. They tell an exciting story of a pilfered legacy, of attempted poisoning of the son by the mother, of her efforts to strangle him, and provide other colorful details as well concerning this Borgia-like person. Sum total they bolstered the legend of Cecco and gave, if not justification, at least a greater comprehension of the pathological loathing he bore his parents. Yet even without these more outrageous provocations, young Angiolieri's relations with his mother were grim indeed. Today, if the fruits of scholarship have reduced the supposed polychromistic portrait of Lisa Salimbeni to a mere sketch, it is a sketch every bit as devastating as a Daumier might have produced.

The afore-mentioned sonnet beginning, "Babb'e Becchina, l'Amor e mie madre, m'hanno si come tord' a siepe stretto," which introduces the mother for the first time in the *Canzoniere,* carries these six lines as its conclusion:

> Mia madr'è lassa per la non potenza
> si ch'i'lo debb'aver per ricevuto,
> da po' ch'i'so la sua malavoglienza.
>
> L'altier passa' per vi'e dièll'un saluto,
> per disaccar la sua mal'accoglienza:
> si disse — Cecco, va', che sie fenduto.
>
> My mother is weary of her inability (to do me harm)
> Though I might as well consider she had done
> Ever since I've known of her ill will toward me.
> The other day I passed her in the street and gave her
> Greeting, just to forestall her hostile word:
> She said, "Cecco, be off, would you were cut in twain!"
>
> (LXXXV)

The ellyptical references to the ill she sought to do him, as well as her bloodthirsty greeting, suggest an affinity to the rejected sonnets, or at least to comparable productions of Angiolieri himself. Mother figures next in the infamous fire sonnet, but as space was not available for the elaboration of a more exquisite torture she is put in the same nameless limbo with father, scorned by life and death alike. (Viz. LXXXVI)

The limitations of Cecco's thematic repertory strike the reader as they presumably struck his listeners. In a relatively mild sonnet the burden of which is that he is simply tired to death of seeing persons rich who ought to be poor and vice versa, the opening lines are, however, curiously significant with regard to the mother:

> Tant'abbo di Becchina novellato
> E di mia madr'e di babbo e d'Amore
> ch'una parte del mondo n'ho stancato.
>
> I've related so much about Becchina
> And about my mother, father and of Love
> That I've wearied a lot of people. (XCVIII)

Note again the introductory line: "So much have I related of Becchina and of my mother." The very fact that the mother receives equal billing with Becchina, father and Love suggests that his listeners had met with her on other occasions. One cannot but speculate as to the existence of lost sonnets. The line also prompts one to question still the assignment of certain of the poems. Indeed, a recent study by Anna Razzini, "Intorno all'autenticità delle rime ascritte a Cecco Angiolieri," *Filologia Romanza*, I fasc. 4, 1954, pp. 30-38, would reassign with considerable assurance to Angiolieri two sonnets which of late have been included in the probable production of Meo dei Tolomei. These are numbers V and VI in Vitale's *Rimatori dell 200 e 300* which treat respectively of the mother's attempts to give bad dietary advice to the ailing poet, and subsequently to poison him.

c) INCIDENTAL THEMES

For the sake of convenience the sonnets relating to love and to money and family have been grouped together since there is some discernable development in each category. The remaining poems, which treat of a variety of themes, include some notable items. As previously observed, it is disappointing that, for the most part, no chronological order can be assigned for we might learn more of our evasive rascal. As it is, however, the sonnets under this miscellaneous rubric, do reveal interesting facets of his nature and talent. With the demise of Angiolieri senior, Cecco, as might be expected, enjoys a brief period of prosperity. His material state, alas, has little influence on his disposition. Far from mitigating his attitude toward the world at large it merely enhances his cockiness. In XCIX he has a go at his erstwhile companions, to whit, the scum of Siena with whom he had so recently associated. He had

evidently been subjected to some raillery, and is quick to pick up
the cudgels. It is a fairly repellent little piece:

>   I' non vi miro perzar, morditori,
>   ch'i' mi conduca ma' nel vostro stato,
>   che 'l dì vi fate di mille colori
>   innanzi che 'l volaggio sia contato.
>
>   Ciò era vostra credenza, be' signori,
>   per ch'i' m'avesse a sollazzo giocato,
>   ch'i divenisse de' frati minori,
>   di non toccar dena' picciol né lato?
>
>   M'assa' ve ne potrà scoppiar lo cuore,
>   ch'i ho saputo sì dìciar e fare,
>   ch'i' ho del mi' assa' dentro e di fore.
>
>   Ma 'l me' ch'i' ho, e che miglior mi pare,
>   sì è 'l veder di vo' che ciascun muore;
>   ché vi convien, per viver, procacciare.

I ignore your jibes, you slanderers.
You'll never reduce me to your state,
You who tremble every day with fright
As your knaveries and pilferings come to light.
Was it not your belief, fine sirs,
Since I jokingly wagered
That not having small cash or hope of any
I might have become a humble friar?
Forthwith may your hearts burst with envy
Since I'm now able to announce
That I've quite sufficient in pocket and in purse.
But a better thing for me — in fact, the best
Would be to see you croak
Because alive you're only birds of prey.

(XCIX)

Sonnet Exchange with Dante

In 1288, Cecco, in company with his father, was one of a contingent sent by Siena to aid the Florentines in their battle against the Ghibellines at Arezzo. Cecco evidently made the acquaintance of Dante here. We know of the relationship only through three sonnets of Cecco. There may have been others, but they, like the replies of Dante, have been lost. Fortunately the three of Cecco appear to be critical milestones in their association. They are completely different in tone and attitude, and bespeak an acquaintance extending over some years. A common interest in letters presumably drew the two together initially. Both were young and in their brief encounter the fundamental difference of their natures was not uncomfortably apparent. In the earliest of the three sonnets, Cecco, after noting that he is weary of poetizing about Becchina,[4] sets out in a most aimiable mood to entertain the Florentine with a brilliantly satiric portrait of an Angevine marshal unquestionably known to both of them. Cecco is aware that Dante will enjoy his effort and one senses that he is sharing a malicious bit of spoofing with a sympathetic companion. The atmosphere is one of pleasant camraderie.

> Lassar vo' lo trovare di Becchina,
> Dante Alighieri, e dir del mariscalco:
> ch'e' par fiorin d'or, ed è di ricalco;
> par zuccar caffettin, ed è salina;
>
> par pan di grano, ed è di saggina;
> par una torre, ed è un vil balco;
> ed è un nibbio, e par un girfalco;
> e pare un gallo, ed è una gallina.
>
> Sonetto mïo, vàtene a Fiorenza:
> dove vedrai le donne e le donzelle,
> di' che 'l su' fatto è solo di parvenza.
>
> Ed eo per me ne conterò novelle
> al bon re Carlo conte di Provenza,
> e per sto mo' gli fregiarò la pelle.

To songs about Becchina here's a halt,
For, Dante, of the Marshal I would treat:
A golden florin? why, he's counterfeit;
Pure Caffa-sugar? no, he's made of salt.
He's bread of maize, for all he would be wheat;
A hut that seems a tower at first sight:
A falcon, sir? he's but a common kite;
A crowing cock? a clucking hen, I ween.

---

[4] It has also been suggested that the sonnet is in reply to one from Dante urging Cecco to find a worthier subject for his talents than Becchina. In any case the advice was not heeded.

Now up, my Sonnet, go to Florence town,
Where dainty dames and damsels you will see:
Expound he's all a sham, and nothing more.
Meanwhile of him some tales I'm jotting down
For good King Carlo of Provence; so we
May rub the wretch's skin till he be sore.

C (Scott)

The gentleman in question has not been positively identified. Del Lungo argues persuasively that he is one Diego de la Rat.[5] Massera inclines to the view that he was rather Amerigo di Narbona, a handsome but inept military man who held a conspicuous post in Florence for some years.

In the second, the atmosphere has changed considerably. Cecco addresses Dante in what seem to be most humble and respectful terms, to advise him that there is an inconsistency in one of his sonnets, *Oltre la sfera che più larga gira*. There is no inconsistency whatever, as Cecco himself knew perfectly well. His sly deceit merely gives him a fine opportunity to attack with quite devastating irony the over subtlizations of the poets of the *dolce stil nuovo*. It is an elegant job of counterfeiting the courtly style. Despite Marti's contention that the sonnet is directed at the excesses of the school, it has a personal animus which cannot be minimized. Alighieri and Angiolieri were, after all, at opposite poles on every score. The Florentine would scarcely have lent himself to this type of malign assault; the Sienese knew no such scruples.

Dante Alighier, Cecco, 'l tu' serv'e amico,
si raccomand'a te com'a segnore;
e sì ti prego per lo dio d'Amore,
il qual è stat'un tu' signor antico,

che mi perdoni s'ispiacer ti dico,
ché mi dà sicurtà 'l tu' gentil cuore;
quel ch'i' ti dico, è di questo tenore:
ch'al tu' sonetto in parte contraddico.

Ch'al meo parer ne l'una muta dice
che non intendi su' sottil parlare,
a que' che vide la tua Beatrice;

---

[5] I. Del Lungo, *I Bianchi e i Neri*, Hoepli, 1921, p. 401 ff.

> e puoi hai detto a le tue donne care
> che tu lo 'ntendi: adunque, contraddice
> a se medesmo questo tu' trovare.
>
> Dante Alighieri, Cecco, your good friend
> And servant, gives you greeting as his lord,
> And prays you for the sake of Love's accord
> (Love being the Master before whom you bend),
> That you will pardon him if he offend,
> Even as your gentle heart can well afford.
> All that he wants to say is just one word
> Which partly chides your sonnet at the end.
> For where the measure changes, first you say
> You do not understand the gentle speech
> A spirit made touching your Beatrice:
> And next you tell your ladies how, straightaway,
> You understand it. Wherefore (look you) each
> Of these your words the other's sense denies.
>
> CI (Rossetti)

As far as is known, Dante never replied to the sonnet, but the jibe was doubtless felt, since he was at pains to explain himself quite specifically when the sonnet was subsequently utilized in the *Vita Nuova*.

Later Dante addresses one or more sonnets to Cecco which, unfortunately are lost. The only reminder of their existence is a thoroughly vituperative piece of Angiolieri which appears to parry point for point what must have been a rousing dressing down which he had received from Dante. Cecco is stung to the quick and lashes forth without measure. The language is coarse, the sentiments are mean. So far as we are aware, Dante himself never deigned to reply, but one Guelf, Taviani, a judge and poet from Pistoia wrote a sharp rebuke to Cecco for his temerity in attacking one of Dante's stature.[6]

Cecco's reply, for all its below-the-belt punches, the allusion to Dante's painful exile, to his dependence upon the hospitality of others — for all its knavishness — it is a splendid bit of invective. The parallelism is deftly carried through, the imagery crude and telling. One has the feeling that the verse was conceived violently and without afterthought. Nothing suggests re-working or polishing.

---

[6] Cf. B. Maier, *Op. cit.*, p. 112.

It has the hot breath of anger and indignation and a liveliness which the centuries have in no way dimmed.

> Dante Alighier, s'i' so bon begolardo,
> tu mi tien' bene la lancia a le reni;
> s'eo desno con altrui, e tu vi ceni;
> s'eo mordo 'l grasso, tu ne sugi 'l lardo;
>
> s'eo cimo 'l panno, e tu vi freghi 'l cardo:
> s'eo so discorso, e tu poco raffreni;
> s'eo gentileggio, e tu misser t'avveni;
> s'eo so fatto romano, e tu lombardo.
>
> Sì che, laudato Deo, rimproverare
> poco pò l'uno l'altro di noi due:
> sventura o poco senno cel fa fare.
>
> E se di questo vòi dicere piùe,
> Dante Alighier, i' t'averò a stancare;
> ch'eo so lo pungiglion, e tu se' 'l bue.

> Dante Alighieri, if I'm a loquacious buffoon
> You're not far behind me,
> If I dine with others, you sup with them too;
> If I gnaw the suet, you suck the fat;
> If I cut the cloth, you card the wool;
> If I'm sharp-tongued, little holds you back;
> If I frequent my betters, your lordship does no less
> I've become a Roman? Well you're a Lombard now.
> The upshot is, may God be praised
> That neither of us can well reproach the other,
> Misfortune and poor judgment made us do it.
> If you've got more to say on this
> Dante Alighieri, I'll wear you down
> For I'm the gad-fly and you're the ox.   (CII)

In many ways this is one of the most remarkable poems in the *Canzoniere*. Apart from an accomplished technical brilliancy, it is, ironically enough, one of the few sonnets in which Angiolieri gives evidence of maturity and a more generous point of view. Life has taught him some lessons and for once there is almost a tone of resignation and wisdom as opposed to canny instinct. The lines:

> Si che, laudato Deo, rimproverare
> poco po' l'uno l'altro di noi due:
> sventura o poco senno cel fa fare.

stand out conspicuously. Dante's attack has brought him to a moment of great lucidity. He is sobered, chastened and humble enough to see himself briefly as he really is. There is no mocking double-talk in these lines but sincerity: "How can one of us reproach the other? We're in the same fix. Tough luck and poor judgment have brought us to this pass." There must have been a passing recollection of friendlier days, almost a gesture of reconciliation; but habits are too ingrained and lest one accuse him of sentimentality, in the final tercet he flips back, true to form, to remind Dante to watch out for he is a still redoubtable adversary.

Of other miscellaneous sonnets, one of the most entertaining is CIII, *Quando Ner Picciolin tornò di Francia*. In this satiric portrait of the Sienese merchant who returns wealthy and arrogant from his ventures in France, Cecco's keen and observant eye is everywhere in evidence. In terms of language and style it is a veritable gem which merits a careful reading. Much the same may be said for the famous *S'i' fosse foco arderei 'l mondo* (LXXXVI) which is so often reproduced in anthologies. Here his extravagant, black humor dominates the piece. From a technical point of view it reveals his craftsmanship at its best and as in the case of the preceding warrants subsequent analysis. There are a few curiously moralizing pieces, quite atypical, and were they not of reputedly secure attribution, one might be tempted to ascribe them to another. We can only suppose that Cecco in a desire to vary his repertory turned to other popular themes as in CIV: *A cosa fatta non vale pentere*, in other words, "Don't cry over spilt milk." It is a little mawkish and self-pitying as is CV:

> Egli è si poco di fede e d'amore
> oggi rimasa fra l'umana gente...
>
> There is so little good will and affection
> Remaining today among us human kind...   (CV)

Perhaps the wine had lost its exhilaration or some upsetting incident had brought him to a pensive mood as he reflects upon changing times and manners. A similar mood colors the following:

> Senno non val a cui Fortuna è conto...
>
> Wisdom won't help you when Fortune has dealt the cards...
>
>   (CVI)

They all reflect the bread and butter philosophy of the tavern, of men who have already passed their first youth. They are common themes of the day and it is not surprising that Cecco tries his hand at them. In workmanship they are competent but not distinguished and one misses the tough bravado which is his hallmark. In a sense, it must be admitted, these three help to round out and humanize this firebrand. We cannot deny him his moments of sober reflection. The sulphuric climaxes demand contrasting periods of relative tranquillity. In the last analysis, however, one wonders how sincere or deeply felt were these reflections. We are too accustomed to Cecco's irreverent about-turns, to his pious exordia which conclude on quite a different note. Our credulity has been tried so often that we remain a little unconvinced.

Related to these versified commentaries on the human condition is a very happy essay at a proverb quite in the best Aesopian tradition which comes off much better. It carries the familiar ring of the poet:

> Stando lo baldovino dentro un prato,
> de l'erba fresca molto pasce e 'nforna;
> vedesi da la spera travallato
> e crede che le orecchie siano corna;
>
> e dice: — Questo fosso d'altro lato
> salterò bene, ch'i' non farò storna —.
> Movesi per saltare lo fossato,
> allor trabocca, e ne lo mezzo torna.
>
> Allora mette un ragghio come tòno:
> — Oimè lasso, che male pensato aggio,
> ché veggio ben che pur asino sono! —
>
> Così del matto avvien, che si cre' saggio;
> ma quando si prova nel parangono,
> al dritto tocco pare il suo visaggio.

Once upon a time within a meadow fair
A donkey roamed, and ate up all he found:
The sunlight cast his shadow on the ground;
He took his ears for horns, so long they were.
— Then I'm in sooth a stag, I do declare;
For further pasture I will jump that brook. —
Straightway his most prodigious leap he took,
And plump into the stream he tumbled there.

> O then he brayed like thunder to the skies: —
> Alack! methought I was of nobler breed,
> Who'm but an ass with two tremendous ears! —
> 'Tis ever thus with fools who think they're wise;
> But truth is proven by the test indeed,
> When what things really are at once appears.
>
> CVII (Scott)

Insofar as the generally accepted sonnets of Angiolieri are concerned, the last item in the standard editions is his response to a request from an otherwise unidentified Simone who seeks advice in combating the tyranny of love. It is light-hearted bit of verse, gracefully and amusingly turned. The advice comes rather as a surprise from one who has never been at a loss in contriving wild and extravagant expedients. It is merely:

> ...non ti lassar romper, ma piegare   (CVIII)

Colloquially turned: "... Don't let it get to you; roll with the punches." Citations from Solomon and Cato bolster his counsel. Thus terminates on a most genial and pacific note the fulminating song cycle of Cecco Angiolieri. The storm has spent itself, the last rumblings of thunder have passed away, the awesome shafts of lightning extinguished. Nature has recomposed herself and order and harmony prevail.

Was it so with Cecco's life? One imagines that the years brought a measure of self-possession and tranquillity to his unbridled soul. There are intimations here and there in the later pieces of a more temperate turn of mind. Were indeed his last years caught up in dulling routine, in the inevitable bending to the exigencies of everyday life? Did he end perhaps inconspicuously as a clerical assistant to the Cardinal Patroni in Rome? Subsequent findings may surprise, but in all likelihood will confirm this supposition. The parabola of his talent moved from its first relatively quiet expression to its clamorous and unruly heights to subside ultimately on a more sobered note. It is essentially a youthful talent, hotblooded and passionate and at its best in dissonant utterance. By the time he had left Siena, his song had indubitably ended.

d) SONNETS OF DUBIOUS ATTRIBUTION

The 20-odd sonnets of dubious attribution have puzzled experts for half a century. As noted previously, the very perceptive work of Adele Todaro in 1935 [7] challenged the authenticity of a number of the sonnets in Massera's compilation. [8] Her work which had elicited almost no comment was taken up in the fifties by Mario Marti [9] whose painstaking efforts confirmed in large part her contentions as well as bringing to light additional material. The net result of their labors was firstly to rehabilitate a hithertoo overlooked poet, Meo dei Tolomei. To this contemporary of Cecco's were assigned with considerable certainty about twenty of the poems; and about twenty were re-assigned tentatively, to Cecco, some with fair certainty, others not. Miss Todaro's efforts, commendable as they had been in forcing a reappraisal were obviously too drastic. As the question now stands, we have a secure corpus of material which is indubitably that of Angiolieri, another which is Meo's and finally a small nest egg which offers tantalizing possibilities to future scholars. To date the "gray area" sonnets appear to reveal no internal evidence which might lead to a more definite assignment; nor have any external data been unearthed which bear upon the problem. The reader is thus still free to indulge in subjective speculation. It is of passing interest to note that even the distinguished Marti has restored to what he considers a definitive selection of Angliolieri's work at least three sonnets which he had previously excluded in his "Sui sonetti attribuiti a Cecco Angiolieri." [10]

---

[7] A. Todaro, *Sull'autenticità dei sonetti attribuiti a Cecco Angiolieri* (Palermo, Scuola tip. "Boccone del Povero" 1934.)

[8] A. F. Massera, *I sonetti di Cecco Angiolieri*, Bologna, Zanichelli, 1906. This edition contained 138 sonnets. Massera subsequently added 12 additional ones. (Viz., *Studi romanzi,* Vol. XIII, 1917, pp. 77-97).

[9] Mario Marti, "Sui sonetti attribuiti a Cecco Angiolieri," *Giornale Storico della Letteratura Italiana,* Vol. 127, 1950, pp. 253-275. In this article he assigns 108 sonnets to Angiolieri. In his *Cultura e stile nei poeti giocosi del tempo di Dante* (Nistri-Lischi, Pisa, 1953), 112 sonnets are ascribed to Angiolieri and 16 are considered of dubious attribution. See also: A. Razzini, "Intorno all' autenticità delle rime ascritte a C.A.," *Filologia romanza,* a.I, fasc. 4 (1954), pp. 30-38.

[10] *Ibid.*

Of the "gray area" sonnets which may be Cecco's or not, four treat of homosexuality. These are the most contentious and the most open to doubt. Curiously enough, in the earlier editions when it was assumed that the lurid tales of the mother, the several allusions to male lovers, as well as other savorous bits were all the work of Angiolieri, the total picture was accepted without question and one sensational fact more or less had little shock value. Since the subtraction from his legacy of certain of these sonnets and the emergence of Meo dei Tolomei to share a portion of the garrish trappings, there has been a reluctance on the part of Italian critics to admit any possible deviation on Cecco's part. Vitale characterizes the sonnets as *materia scabrosa* [11] adding that there is no proof that the poet had any such inclinations. Yet expert opinion hesitates to assign the poems to Meo or to another and they remain in the manuscript copies amidst others of Cecco's. As yet no answer is forthcoming.

Frequently when authorship is thus in question, a definite majority of those familiar with the writer share an intuitive conviction as to the authenticity of certain productions. Such is not the case with these poems. They are a baffling phenomenon, indeed, which repeated perusal does nothing to clarify. In tone and workmanship they suggest Cecco, yet a Cecco who is a little unfamiliar to us. After the passionate outpourings to Becchina, the reader is somewhat taken aback to discover that the recipient of these verses is the pink-cheeked boy, the cruel Corso di Corazon, or his attractive companion. To be sure, such sentiments, though no more in favor than any other period, were prevalent enough at the time. Witness the allusions in the contemporary verse to the subject. Obviously there is nothing in Angiolieri's life to suggest moral scruples, continence or any other deterrent which might render such experiences repugnant. He is an unabashed hedonist, his favorite haunt the tavern, his companions among Siena's least desirable.

Virtually nothing in the *Canzoniere* gives any hint of inverted tastes unless one were to question the deep sense of shame and degradation which is encountered in certain of the sonnets on poverty. Cecco's poverty was a relative thing. His family, after all, was

---

[11] M. Vitale, *Rimatori comico-realistici del due e trecento* (Torino, 1956), p. 446 ff.

conspicuously well-to-do, and strained as were family relations, it is unlikely that he would have been permitted to starve. One recalls that according to Boccaccio's account, the father had outfitted the son quite presentably so that he might take his place in the cardinal's suite. It is an apocryphal story, perhaps, but still part of the accepted legend. Cecco himself notes that:

> ...mi fu dato
> per mia ristorazion moglie
>
> ...and there was given me
> for my recovery — a wife   (LXXX)

The securing of a wife to set him on the straight road was evidence of some concern; and doubtless there were many other instances when the family, if only to save face, lent a helping hand and assuredly would have done more to a different type of offspring. Nevertheless in the poverty sonnets there are indications that the poet considered himself a pariah and suffered from undue sensitivity, feeling, for example, that he was the cynosure of all eyes as he walked the streets:

> O lasso me...
> da poi che la ventura m'è si scorsa
> ch'andando per la via ogn'uom m'addita
>
> Unhappy that I am...
> since fortune has abandoned me
> When I walk along the streets every man points at me
> (LXX)

In colorful lines which were previously noted in a different context, one is struck by the poet's debasement. It has a ring of sincerity:

> Son più vil che non fu pro' Tristano
> e 'nfra le genti vo col capo 'n seno
> più vergognoso ch'un can foretano
>
> I am more vile than Tristan was courageous,
> And walk among the crowd with head hung low
> More shameful than a homeless cur...   (LXXV)

The same sentiment is echoed again in LXXVI:

> Allor mi stringo com'in nave stiva
> ed in la cera tutto mi nascondo...
>
> Then I make myself as inconspicuous as can be
> And hide my face to the best of my ability...   (LXXVI)

There is something a little morbid and unhealthy in these lines which temporary poverty does not entirely explain.[12] The question of Cecco's sincerity might well be raised again. Are these simply examples of his penchant for the highly colored phrase, for the breast-beating rhetoric which is his stock-in-trade? Perhaps they are, yet re-readings seem to convey a deeper note of self pity. One feels that, as in the Becchina sonnets, these may well be the fitful flashes of genuine emotion which quite involuntarily reveal for a fleeting second the real Cecco, shorn of his bravado.

One is reminded also of a passing comment in another sonnet:

> ...mi son frustato
> di tutti i vizi che solìa avere
> non m'è rimasto se non quel di bere.
>
> ...I've given up
> All the vices I used to have
> save that of drinking.   (LXV)

What, indeed, were "all the vices" to which he alludes? Is there not the barest possibility that they included homosexuality which did brand him and occasion much of the humiliation which is difficult to substantiate on the grounds of poverty alone. The argument is manifestly too tenuous to force, but represents about the only internal evidence which can be brought to bear on the question.

Had the love object in the first of the poems treating of homosexuality been Becchina or another of her sex the sonnet might well pass for Cecco's. From its arresting opening to its casual even sardonic adoption of courtly expression to its extravagant conclusion, it is plausibly in his style and might have occasioned no particular

---

[12] Marti sees shame of poverty as a typical attitude of poets of the comic school. M. Marti, *Op. cit.*, p. 87.

question were it not for "cotal c'ha'l volto di tre bei colori," that is, the fresh-complexioned young man. It should be noted in passing that "i tre bei colori," namely white, vermilion and rose, were the colors conventionally used to describe feminine beauty in those distant days before peach and bronze hues equaled or surpassed them in acceptability. To find them applied to this youth is a transposition which brings the reader up smartly with the question of authorship. At this point the answer can only be conjecture. Here is the first, Number CXXIII. Let the reader make of it what he will:

    — Udite udite, dico a voi, signori,
    e fate motto, voi che siete amanti:
    avreste voi veduto, tra cotanti,
    cotal c'ha 'l volto di tre be' colori?

    Di ros'e bianch'e vermigli'è di fuori;
    or lo mi dite, ch'i' vi son davanti,
    sed elli inver di me fe' tai sembianti,
    ched i' potessi aver que' suo' colori.

    — Noi non crediam che li potessi avere,
    però ched e' non fece ta' sembianti,
    che fosse ver' di te umilïato.

    — Sed e' nol fece, i' mi pongo a giacere
    e comincio a far ta' sospiri e pianti,
    che 'n quattro dì cred'esser sotterrato.

Hear, hear, I speak to you good sirs.
Give me answer, you who are lovers.
Have you seen among those yonder
That chap whose face is so fresh and fair,
Rose, white, vermilion beyond compare?
Tell me as I stand before you
If, concerning me, he's ever given sign
That I might possess those charms?
We don't believe you can
For he's never given any indication
That he is well disposed towards you.
Well, if he won't, I'll throw myself down
And give forth with such sighs and moans
That in four days I'll be underground.   (CXXIII)

The introduction and conclusion of the second again suggest Angiolieri, though elsewhere there is a slightly whiney, feminine tone that admittedly is very hard to associate with the poet.

>   I' so non fermo in su questa oppenione
>   di non amar, a le sante guagnele,
>   uomo che sia inver di me crudele,
>   non abbiendo egli alcuna cagione;
>
>   ma questo dico, sanza riprensione,
>   di non servirti, né sarò fedele,
>   poi che di dolce mi vòi render fele:
>   fàilti tu, ma non ne hai ragione.
>
>   Da ch'i' conosco la tua sconoscenza,
>   che tu ricredente contra me fai,
>   vogli'arrestare di te mai servire.
>
>   Per la qual cosa i' crederei 'nsanire,
>   se tu non n'avessi gran penitenza,
>   con essa avendo grandissimi guai.
>
> I'm not firm in my resolution
> To love or not, despite the holy scriptures,
> A man who is so cruel towards me —
> And without any reason.
> But this I say, quite without regret
> I'm not your slave nor will I faithful be
> Since you return my love with spite.
> You do indeed, and without provocation.
> Since I've learned of the ingratitude
> Which you so wrongly show toward me
> No longer do I wish to be your friend.
> Were you to show repentance
> And with it some just grief,
> I'd think I'd lost my mind.   (CXXIV)

It would be a Cecco completely mesmerized by this lover to write:

>   ...dico...
>   di non servirti, ne sarò fedele
>   poi che di dolce mi voi render fele
>   ... ...
>
>   Da ch'i' conosco la tua sconoscenza,
>   che tu ricredente contra me fai

Even the concluding wish that he who has caused the poet's anguish be forced to suffer "grandissimi guai" is a much mollified and feminized version of the usual blood and thunder imprecations which Cecco is wont to distribute. And yet, he may well have been so under his spell that for the moment his masculinity is in abeyance. The two addressed to the unidentified Corzo di Corzan — and we assume that Corzo and Corso are one and the same — speak for themselves:

>   Un Corzo di Corzan m'ha sì trafitto,
> che non mi val cecèrbita pigliare,
> né dolci medicine né amare,
> né otrïaca che vegna d'Egitto.
>
>   E ciò che Galïen ci lasciò scritto
> aggio provato per voler campare:
> tutto m'è gocciola d'acqua nel mare,
> tanto m'ha 'l su' velen nel mie cor fitto.
>
>   Là 'nd'i' son quasi al tutto disperato,
> poi ched e' non mi val null'argomento;
> a questo porto Amor m'ha arrivato.
>
>   Ché son quell'uom, che più vivo sgomento,
> che si' nel mondo o che mai fosse nato:
> chi me n'ha colpa, di terra sia spento.

One Corso from Corzan's so wounded me
That naught avails the healingest herbs there are,
Nor medicines that sweet or bitter be:
Nor theriac that comes from Egypt far.
I've read Galen's writings thoroughly
And in them nothing found to ease my pains.
They're like one drop of water in the sea
So deeply runs the poison in my veins.
Because of this I have grown desperate
Since no persuasion any power has.
To this port Love has brought me, my sails furled.
I live more shaken — that is my sad fate —
Than any man there is or ever was.
Who's wronged me, May God take him from this world.

CXXV (Chubb)

Guerri makes the ingenious suggestion that Corzo is a rival of Cecco's and the sonnet is one of jealousy and anger.[13] If the sonnet is, indeed, Cecco's and Cecco is "straight," then the object of the two gentlemen's affection is a lady and all is well. Such is manifestly not the case in the second where the happy recipient of their attention is the *gaio compagno*. If Corzo and Corso are different persons, Guerri's thesis would also conceivably stand, but the juxtaposition of the sonnets in the basic listing and the variant spellings of Corzo and Corso, probably only the calligraphic vagary of the scribe, would seem to render this most unlikely. In CXXV, scarcely proof positive, but at least indicative of Cecco are the reference to Galien, which also occurs in XC (but never in the sonnets of Meo), and the phrase *gocciola d' acqua nel mare* which is found at least twice elsewhere in the *Canzoniere* (XXXV and LXIII).

In the fourth and last of the homosexual sonnets, a variety of emotions is vividly depicted in the small canvas. Love, hate, jealousy and revenge sputter forth, and though Cavalli in his commentary professes to find nothing angiolieresque therein, this would seem a difficult position to maintain. The vengeful tone, the similes, the mocking twist at the end are very much in the manner of Cecco. To be sure, no further assertion would be prudent, and the question still remains very much an open one.

> In tale, che d'amor vi passi 'l core,
> abbattervi possiate voi, ser Corso,
> e sì vi pregi vie men ch'un vil torso
> e come tòsco li siate in amore.
>
> E facciavi mugghiare a tutte l'ore
> del giorno, come mugghia bue od orso,
> e, come l'ebbro bee a sorso a sorso
> il vin, vi facci ber foco e martore.
>
> E se non fosse ch'i' non son lasciato,
> sì mal direi, e vie più fieramente,
> al vostro gaio compagno e avvenente
>
> che di bellezze avanzan ogni uom nato;
> ma sì mi stringe l'amor infiammato,
> che verso lui ho sparto per la mente.

---

[13] D. Guerri, "Cecco Angiolieri: Revisone delle rime del 'Beffardo', *Rivista di sintessi letteraria*, I, n. 3, 1934, pp. 419-436.

> May you, Ser Corso, meet with some one who
> Shall rouse your heart to serve his every whim;
> As some old cabbage may he reckon you,
> And may your love be poison unto him:
> And may he make you roar throughout the day,
> Like any bull or bear that knows no shame,
> And as the drunkard sips his wine away,
> May you be forced to drink of liquid flame.
> Were I not bridled now to some degree,
> Much more I'd add, with even greater scorn,
> About your gay companion fair and free,
> Surpassed in looks by none of woman born;
> But I'll refrain, altho' I feel inclined:
> An ardent love for him yet fills my mind.
>   CXXVI (Scott)

The four sonnets are in any case, very effectively turned and reminiscent in texture and phraseology of Cecco. Alas, more cannot be said. They may reflect a period of aberration in his life; they may possibly be the work of another, but at least one who was not dissimilar from Cecco in his talents.

Of the remaining "dubious" sonnets a few are rather routine productions devoid of any characteristics which might provide a clue to authorship. Except for their presence amid others of Cecco and Meo, they might have been turned out by almost any of the contemporary poets of the school (e.g. CXIII, CXVII, CXIX, CXX). Others, however, have a stamp of originality which invites attention. They have been so long associated with Angiolieri that in the absence of strong testimony to the contrary they will probably remain attached to his name. Among these, CXI could, with no stretch of the imagination, be included amongst those berating Becchina for her cruelties. It begins:

> Maladetto e distrutto sia da Dio
> lo primo punto ch'io innamorai
> di quella che dilettasi di guai
> darmi, ed ogni altro sollazzo ha in oblío...
>
> Cursed and annihilated by God
> Be that first moment when I fell in love
> With that girl who delights in giving me
> Such pain and withholds every other solace...

It is a forceful bit, and if not Angiolieri's would seem to be a shameless imitation. Indeed, Marti now has no hesitation in numbering it amongst Cecco's.[14] It might be noted, too, that Meo's repertory contains nothing remotely similar in subject or treatment.

Number CXII finds Italian critics reluctant to ascribe it to the poet essentially because of its "obscene" turn. One wonders if Angiolieri warrants such delicate reservation. The comic school is full of obscenities and there is little reason to suppose that this forthright and blunt Cecco whose tongue is never curbed, might not have slipped over the edges on occasion himself. The sonnet, a stag party number, is a delightful parody on courtly verse, which after all was a specialty of Cecco's. The opening lines set the mood:

> S'i'potesse d'amico in terzo amico
> contare a la mia donna, con onore,
> lo core mio stando servidore...
>
> Could I but through a series of friends
> Advise my lady that most honorably
> My heart stands at her service...

The exordium is a dead give-away. In the world of the *cavaliere servente,* where secrecy and mystery were *de rigueur,* the poet would use the grapevine approach to his lady's ear. The stereotyped elegancies of the aulic school are then pressed to service to express the lover's desire to guard with his honor his lady's private parts. He concludes rapturously that beside her Helen of Troy would not have such appeal were hers encrusted with emeralds and rubies. It is a vulgar little piece, but amusing and not in the least beyond Cecco's pen had it suited his purpose.

Number CXV, a jolly verse in praise of money, seems to bear the angiolieresque touch, though admittedly the theme was so common that any of his admirers might have written it:

> I buoni parenti, dica chi dir vuole
> a chi ne puo aver, sono i fiorini...
>
> Good parents, say what you will,
> For him who has them, are florins...

---

[14] M. Vitale, *Op. cit.,* p. 433.

Make no mistake, he avers, money is your best escutcheon. With it you have everything, material possessions, friends and esteem. If a man has the tough luck to be poor, he might as well admit: "Io nacqui come fungo a'tuoni e venti" (I was born like a mushroom in the wind and the rain). The sentiments, so often expressed by the comic school, are, however, sufficiently reminiscent in tone and in turn of phrase to Cecco (Cf. LXVI and LXVII), especially the telling metaphor of the last line cited above, that it requires little persuasion to include this in his poverty cycle.

Number CXVI, "Con gran malinconia istò" an ingenious *tour de force* in which each line ends in an accented vowel after the manner of the Sicilian and Guittonian schools is a fine sonnet, whoever its author may have been. Technically it would have appealed to Cecco as a literary feat. In fact, it has superficial parallels with Number IV, "Oimè d'Amor, che m'è duce si reo," in which each line begins with *Oimè,* making thus a sort of reverse pattern to the present sonnet. Curiously enough it also contains a reference to his melancholy: "oimè, ch'eo n'ho pure malinconia." And, be it noted, Number CXVI concludes with the word: *Omè*. Perhaps pure coincidence, perhaps an author's recall conscious or otherwise; but Italian criticism is hesitant in assigning it to Angiolieri essentially because the uneasy *malinconia* which it describes harks more to a romantic tradition than to the dour, frustrated melancholy which Cecco consistently depicts. Nonetheless, a careful reading of No. CXVI in conjuntion with others which express his melancholy (e.g. No's IV, X, etc.) scarcely seems to reveal any very fundamental difference in mood. On the contrary one is struck rather by the similarity of tone amongst them. While Cavalli and Vitale abstain from final judgment, Marti has ultimately opted for Cecco; and in the light of the curious parallels mentioned above, his decision seems entirely tenable.

There are two rather heavy-handed satires of military life, to whit, No's. CXXII and CXXX which voice a soldier's exaggerated complaints of food and general conditions and sound much like any articulate and sarcastic draftee. In view of Cecco's own lack-luster military career, he might well have been prompted to write them, but their very texture scarcely suggests his pen. Furthermore, Number CXXX begins:

> Salute manda lo tu' Buon Martini,
> Berto Rinier, de la putente Magna
>
> Your pal, Buon Martini, sends greetings,
> Berto Rinier, from stinking Germany.

Ostensibly one Martini, perhaps Buon Martini, otherwise unidentified, is its author. Berto Ranieri, the recipient, was, according to Massera, a distant relative of the Angiolieri family. But nowhere else has Cecco used the device of feigned authorship; there is nowhere any other reference to Ranieri, and one doubts very much that Cecco had any acquaintance with Germany. The fact that these two unlikely sonnets were found among Cecco's is perplexing, but so were those of Meo.

Number CXXI, a well-known sonnet which has elicited considerable comment because of its saucy theme, could conceivably have come from the pen of Meo dei Tolomei or from Cecco's. Marti assigns it, though with reservations, to the former; but a rereading of Meo's sonnets leaves one with the distinct impression that his talents are not on the same level as those of Cecco. The poems are thinner in content, the pungent lines fewer, and his similes and metaphors are rarely as picturesque and telling as those of Angiolieri. In this, the images of the bear and porcupine are purely in the vein of the latter, as is the perfectly sustained dialogue. Even the final "punch line" as it were, is a specialty of Cecco. It is an amusing, completely unselfconscious piece, notably well-turned.

> L'altrier sì mi ferìo una tal ticca,
> ch'andar mi fece a madonna di corsa:
> andava e ritornava com'un'orsa
> che va arrabbiando e 'n luogo no si ficca.
>
> Quando mi vide, credett'esser ricca;
> disse: — Non avrestù cavelle in borsa? —
> Rispuosi: — No —. Quella mi disse: — Attorsa,
> e lèvala pur tosto, o tu t'impicca! —
>
> Mostravas'aspra come cuoio di riccio;
> e' le feci una mostra di moneta:
> quella mi disse: — Avesti caporiccio? —
>
> Quasi beffava e stava mansueta,
> che l'avari' tenuta un fil di liccio;
> ma pur ne venni con la borsa queta.

THE SONNETS

> The other day I was struck with such an urge
> That I went dashing to my lady.
> I rushed about just like a bear,
> So full of zest I couldn't wait.
> When she saw me, thinking me well-heeled
> She said, "You've something in your purse?"
> "No," said I. "Get out," said she,
> "And fast, or you'll get what's coming"
> She was as prickly as a porcupine.
> When I showed my cash, how fast she changed.
> "You're in the mood" she queried.
> She began to kid, and was so sweet
> That I could have had her on a leash—
> When I returned my purse was limp.
>
> (CXXI)

Similarly meriting comment is Number CXXVIII, a sonnet remarkable as one of the first in which a variety of dialectical forms are put to comic use:

> Pelle chiabelle di Dio, no ci arvai,
> poi che feruto ci hai l'omo di Roma.
> I' son da Lucca. Che di'? che farai?
> Porto cocosse a vender una soma.
>
> Doi te gaitivo, u' di' che 'nde vai?
> Entro 'gn'Arezzo, a vender queste poma.
> Quest'àscina comprai da' barlettai
> entro 'n Pistoia e féi tonder la chioma.
>
> De' che ti dea 'l malan, fi' de la putta,
> ch'a Firenze n'ha' sèrique a danaio,
> ed ancor più, e giugnet'u' mellone.
>
> A le guagnele! carich'è 'l somaio,
> e porta a Siena a vender cheste frutta,
> sì fuoron colte di buona stagione.

> By the Holy Nails! you shall not get away!
> You've struck a Roman, I would have you know.—
> I come from Lucca: what's your will, I say?—
> Pumpkins I sell, a pack-full can I show.—
> You cheating rascal! where d'ye think to go?—
> Ripe pippins from Arezzo! buy, who'll buy!—
> Some coopers had this moke: I bought her so,
> And hogged her mane: yes, Pistoiese am I.—

> Be damned to you, you whoreson! why, you'd ask
> In Florence for a dozen such, and more,
> One penny, and add a melon too in reason. —
> Now by the Gospels, I have done my task;
> My donkey's laden with a goodly store
> Of fruit for Siena, gathered in due season. —
>
> CXXVIII (Scott)

The scene is a market place with a babel of voices as Roman, Florentine, Sienese, and other vendors go about their business each giving utterance to some characteristic turn of phrase which reveals his regional speech habits. It is the type of rapid patter which Cecco handles so felicitously. In this instance it is orchestrated with extraordinary skill and concision. But how to render it in English? One might imagine a Cockney, a Yorkshire farmer, a cotton picker from Alabama, a Bronx peddler and a few others jabbering away. Their commonplace observations ebb and flow, climax and resolve to form a tiny symphony. In the Chigiano manuscript the sonnet is anonymous. But compare it to the opening sonnet of the Canzoniere: "Accorri, accorri, accorri, uom, a la strada!" and to No. XXII, "Becchina mia — Cecco, nol ti confesso". The brilliant repartee is essentially the same, with réliques literally bristling throughout the fourteen lines. All share in common a marvelous theatrical quality which is Cecco's particular trademark. With Meo, while effective passages occur, the whole texture, as previously noted, is consistently weaker. The brio, the rythmn and color never quite attain the same level that is encountered in Cecco. The author is obviously an artist of great technical ability and the only likely candidate is Angiolieri.

The sonnets in this group present a curious phenomenon. For centuries they have lain peaceably amongst the many others of Cecco and Meo. Yet even after years of critical appraisal, scholars cannot in good conscience assign them to either poet, nor gainsay that they may not even be the work of an unknown whose verse found its way, who knows how, into one of the manuscripts. At this late date, it is exceedingly unlikely that a fortuitous literary windfall will shed further light upon the puzzling questions which they present. From the foregoing discussion, however, some fragile scraps of evidence would seem to tip the balance in Cecco's favor in a few instances. In others, Meo, or an unknown, would appear the more likely author.

CHAPTER III

STYLE AND TECHNIQUE

If Angiolieri's repertory is meager, his technical resources are of a very high order. In all of Italian literature one encounters no more original nor personal style. His presentations consistently surpass their content. As one may readily appreciate from the foregoing discussion, lofty themes and elevated thoughts held no appeal for Cecco. His concerns rarely go beyond the mundane. Sex, money, the desire to amuse, to astound and shock, plus a little home-spun philosophizing cover his thematic range. No need to reiterate that the presentations excel in terms of sheer entertainment, and in a notably brilliant use of the emergent Italian tongue. Trucchi's comment of some 130 years ago still remains a most perceptive one in characterizing Cecco's manner of poetizing as *nova, scellerata ed empia, ma energica*,[1] "new, knavish, impious, but lively." Indeed these words very nearly sum up the discernable ingredients of his sparkling and savorous handling of the idiom. Pirandello in a critical study, "I Sonetti di Cecco Angiolieri,"[2] apparently much intrigued by the work of his early compatriot, devoted a number of pages to a consideration of his language. Pointing to the unsettled state of the Italian tongue at this time, he notes quite rightly that Cecco is in the privileged position of being able to make use almost indiscriminately of a vast variety of linguistic forms to achieve his effects. Sapegno in commenting upon Cecco's language remarks similarly:

---

[1] F. Trucchi, *Op. cit.* Vol. I, p. 271.
[2] Luigi Pirandello, *Saggi* (Milano, 1952), pp. 289 ff.

Osserviamo la sua lingua, la quale non è, come fu detto "pretto senese"; bensì una creazione composta, costituita nel fondo d'elementi attinti al volgare letterario, che s'andava proprio in quegli anni stabilmente configurando, e arricchita poi di parole e frasi tolte al gergo di Siena a scelte con quel gusto amoroso del vocabolo vivo, calzante e sonóro, che ha distinto in ogni tempo certi scrittori di Toscana.[3]

The admixture of the learned tongue with the popular is a comic device which has been used from time immemorial. As previously noted, one of the prime sources of the poets of the comico-realist school was Goliardic verse, not only in its themes of wine, women, money, fortune, and the like, but in its lexicon which mixed with satiric intent the literary tongue with the raciest of common parlance. The *Farce de Maître Pathelin* employs to some extent this device, as does Molière many years later not to mention countless others. Linguistic miscegenation has always held an irresistible appeal. In the hands of a knowing manipulator it can be remarkably effective. Cecco is the first in Italian letters to apply this formula.[4]

The work of Cecco's contemporaries, of course, reflects much of the same linguistic richness, or chaos, as you will; but none profited from the situation in quite the same fashion. The language specialist finds in Angiolieri alone a fascinating showcase of the phonology and morphology of the Italian language at one of the most interesting moments in its development. It has adolescent grace and awkwardness, charm and absurdity as it stumbles between latinisms and the vernacular. Usage, syntax, form and spelling are still in an engagingly inchoate state. The sonnets abound in thinly disguised Latin forms which stubbornly persist at this time (to the delight of the philologist). Note for example:

---

[3] Natalino Sapegno, *Il Trecento* (Milano, 1955), p. 86. "Observe his language, which is not, as has been said, pure Sienese but rather a composite creation constituted basically of elements drawn from the literary idiom which was in those years gradually establishing itself, and enriched then with words and phrases taken from popular Sienese speech, words chosen with that sure taste for the lively, the relevant and the sonorous which has always characterized certain Tuscan writers."

[4] Georgio Petrocchi, "I Poeti realistici," in *Storia della Letteratura Italiana*, a cura di Emilio Cecchi e Natalino Sapegno (Milano, 1965), I, p. 691.

STYLE AND TECHNIQUE   85

bontate, degnitate, povertate, veritate, vertute, parvanza, temenza

to say nothing of an occasional encounter with:

appo, ita, enfra, sed

Duplicative and interchangeable verb forms occur in profusion. Cecco has at his disposal such alternatives as:

ho, abbo, aggio   dirabbo, dirò
fora, saria, sarebbe, fie   prenderaggio, prenderò
fi, fia, sarà   savesse, sapesse
fo, fu   cherrei, chiederei
porria, potrebbe   vorrie, vorrei
pon, possono   veggiono, vedono
vegno, vengo

What an accommodation to the sonneteer in search for an elusive rime or an extra syllable! Orthography and pronunciation are anything but standardized, and the prevalence of dialectical forms simply gives greater scope to this diversity. Who at this point in linguistic history can red pencil the individual vagaries of any writer? Thus, Cecco can with impunity write:

eo, el di, lialmente, manera, pregione, oppinion, or oppenione, semana or settimana, om, omini

to cite at random. Appocopation and elision are constantly encountered. Syllables pour forth in profusion as his nimble tongue trips from consonant to consonant quite unmindful of the intervening vowels. Occasionally it can prove somewhat baffling:

che 'l mi' coraggio
io vorre' 'nanzi 'n grazia ritornare
tu se' me' che 'l pane

Initial and final *i*'s are a favorite target:

'mperador, 'mpiccare, 'nanzi, 'nteso, 'nd, ma', co', e', da', que'

At the same time prosthetic forms appear with almost equal frequency:

> enemico, emmantinente, escusato, ispiacer, isperanza, ista, istornare

One would be quite at a loss to deduce any conventional notions of grammar or usage from Angiolieri's practice. *Che* is employed interchangeably with *ca, cad,* or *ched*; *chi* may stand for *qui*; *chel* and *cheste* for *quel* and *queste.* We come upon *chiu* for *più. Li* equates with *gli* or *le,* and *elli* with *egli* or *essi.* And occasionally the exuberant poet with his penchant for extravagant phraseology appears to create his own vocabulary with superlatives such as:

> trasvolentieri, trasamare, trarripare, desamorare, non discredo, etc.

In the midst of his racy chatter one's attention is occasionally arrested by allusions of seemingly literate import. He refers airily to Cato, Hippocrates, Solomon, Helen of Troy and others in such fashion that a random reading of a few sonnets might suggest a background of respectable study. Surely as the son of one of Siena's most conspicuous citizens, it is reasonable to assume that he would have been exposed to the proper education for a youth of his station. A more comprehensive reading of Angiolieri dispels any such notion, however, and suggests rather that he could one day have exclaimed, as did his French counterpart:

> Hé! Dieu, se j'eusse estudié
> Où temps de ma jeunesse folle

His learning is soon revealed to be little more than that which an alert young man might have picked up from quasi-intellectual acquaintances. The names Merlin, Tristan and Helen were very nearly household words in that era. Similarly references to Lucifer, Eve, St. John, Judas and to the few other names from biblical lore disclose no more learning than would be garnered from a benighted parish priest-beyond these nothing but the mention of Mohammed or the Wandering Jew or even a Latin line from Cato's *Disticha,* a text much studied in the schools. Nor is there any subtle allusion in their use, nothing that bespeaks a first-hand knowledge of the *chansons de geste,* or the Bible, or Latin. Cecco's cultural background is notably thin, his knowledge distinctly popular in character. Be this noted rather as observation than criticism, for little did it matter to this talented artist. His particular style supports ill any corpus of bookish learning. One realizes that the allusions which he does make are surprisingly apt, and what is more important, within the ken of his audience.

Add to his masterly handling of the language, with its innate sense of timing, of the *mot juste,* his love of paradox, his inexhaustible taste for hyperbole and impossibles, the funny, vulgar thrusts, the shock-appeal and one has in a sense isolated the essential elements of his style. It is in their particular blend that his genius asserts itself. Consider the picturesque similes which are his stock-in-trade. Most of the more extravagant ones turn naturally upon the subject of love, especially his painful attachment to Becchina. Entirely typical and a veritable gem of sonnet architecture is Number VI quoted below. Love's sickness is the greatest of woes and to throw off its shackles surpasses in difficulty just about everything imaginable.

>   Quanto un granel di panico è minore
>   del maggior monte che abbia veduto;
>   e quanto 'l bon fiorin de l'or migliore
>   di qualunca denaro più minuto;
>
>   e quanto m'è più pessimo el dolore
>   ad averlo, e l'ho, ch'a averlo perduto:
>   cotant'è maggio la pena d'amore,
>   ched io non averei mai creduto.
>
>   Ed or la credo, però ch'io la provo
>   en tal guisa che per l'anima mia,
>   di questo amor vorrìa ancor esser novo.
>
>   Ed ho en disamar quella bailìa
>   c'ha 'l pulcinello ch'è dentro da l'ovo,
>   d'uscir 'nnanzi ched el su' tempo sia.

>   As much as a grain of millet
>   Is smaller than the highest peak,
>   As the good gold florin
>   Exceeds the widow's mite,
>   So much worse to me the sorrow

>Of loving (and I do) than having lost:
>Ah me, never would I have believed
>How terrible the pain of love could be.
>But now I feel it and I know
>Upon my soul, its hurt is such
>That I'd like never to have known.
>I've about as much chance to free myself
>As has a chick within its shell
>To issue forth before his time. (VI)

This is pure Angiolieri with his hyperbolic sufferings; but note the vivid and piquant images:

>c'ha 'l pulcinello ch'è dentro da l'ovo,
>d'uscir 'nnanzi ched el su' tempo sia.

or the *granel di panico* compared to the highest mountain, or the happy interweaving of his words:

>ad averlo, e l'ho, ch'a averlo perduto

It is a simple thought colorfully illustrated within the confines of a strict sonnet form, straightforward in its rime (ab ab ab ab/ bcbcbc) without a superfluous word, brisk-paced and all of a piece. In the next sonnet, Number VII, pursuing the same theme, he has an arresting exordium which must have delighted his auditors:

>Io poterei così star senz amore
>Come la soddomia tòllar a Moco,
>o come Ciampolin gavazzatore
>potesse vivar tollendoli 'l gioco ...

>I could stop loving, as I do
>About as well as Moco could give up sodomy
>Or that guzzler Ciampolin
>Could give up shooting crap. (VII)

The succeeding lines whilst carrying on the argument, make allusion to still more unidentifiable personnages and their weaknesses, until Cecco, very much tongue-in-cheek concludes:

>Però mi facci Amor ciò che li piace,
>ch'i' sarò sempre su'servo fedele
>e sofferrò ciò che mi farà 'n pace;

STYLE AND TECHNIQUE

> e sed e' fosse amaro più che fele
> con l'umiltà ch'è vertù sì verace,
> il farò dolce come cannamele
>
> Let Love do what he will with me.
> I'll always be his faithful slave
> And suffer in peace his assaults;
> And prove they bitter as gall
> I with humility — that noble virtue —
> Will make them sweet as caramel.
>
> (VII)

The ending, certainly a play to his listeners, is the more amusing since Cecco, of all people, was the least disposed to silent suffering and humility. How perfectly this sonnet supports the contention that Angiolieri's work was primarily designed for public entertainment. Surely the very texture indicates oral presentation. It is patently addressed to the tavern crowd with its references to well-known personalities. From start to finish it is calculated to draw laughs, and Cecco, ever the showman, reserves the final billing for himself.

How fond he is of numbers! He announces that his sufferings have assumed such gigantic proportions that:

> Da Giuda in fuor, neuno sciagurato
> fu, né sarà di chi a cento mili 'anni
> ch'a mille miglia m'appressisi a'panni;   (XLVIII)
>
> Since Judas, not a single wretch
> Was, nor will be from now on for 100,000 years
> Who'd approach me within a thousand miles

And similarly:

> Per ogne oncia di carne che ho addosso
> e' ho ben cento libre di tristizia   (LXXIX)
>
> For every ounce of flesh upon me
> I've easily a hundred pounds of woe.

Or in a better mood:

> Per ogne gocciola d'acqua c'ha 'n mare
> ha cento mili' allegrezze 'l meo core   (XXXV)

> For every drop of water in the sea
> I've a 100,000 delights in my heart.

And in the admirable verse depicting his sleepless night, he exclaims:

> Parmi la notte ben cento mili 'ore   (XLIX)

> Night seems like 100,000 hours

The sonnets on poverty contain a rich assortment of colorful expressions ranging from preposterous to ingratiating. Humiliated by his penniless state he confesses:

> E buffo forte e tro di gran sospiri
> e faccio di quelle di Mongibello
> si com'el lupo che non trova carne   (LXXVI)

> I pant and give forth anguished sighs
> And sound like Mt. Etna roaring,
> Or like a wolf that can't find meat

One telling image, often cited, comes from the famous line, later borrowed by Meo dei Tolomei as the beginning of one of his sonnets:

> I' son si magro, che quasi traluco,
> de la persona no, ma de l'avere   (LXXIII)

> I am so thin that I'm almost transparent
> not of my person, but of my possessions

Or the metaphor of the bear:

> ch'e' mi conven far di quelle de l'orsa
> che per la fame si lecca le dita   (LXX)

> I'm reduced to doing like the bear
> Who from hunger licks his paws

The altogether engaging:

> Quando veggio Becchina corrucciata
> se io avesse allor cuor di leone

> si tremarei com'un picciol garzone
> quando 'l maestro gli vuol dar palmata   (VIII)

> When I see Becchina in a huff
> Had I the heart of a lion
> I'd tremble like a craven schoolboy
> When the master would apply his rule

His wife with her nagging is like:

> E 'l su garrir paion mille chitarre   (LXXX)

> Her chattering sounds like a thousand guitars

Though Italian critics have tended to characterize certain passages in Cecco's verse as obscene, in terms of modern day criticism, they seem pretty tame. There is without question, much rough and pithy talk, but it is simply the colorful speech of average men — and common women, if you wish — at street corners, in taverns, in completely natural unguarded conversation. It is vulgar, but in the etymological sense of the word — innocently and spontaneously the speech of people. Unfortunately, for generations, translators have consistently betrayed this speech by reproducing it in literary English, or Victorian English, or with what was deemed to be the proper poetical vocabulary of the day. The marvelous opening sonnet, for example, offers a prelude to what may be subsequently encountered. In answer to the cry, "Help" "Help," the interlocutor responds laconically:

> Che ha' fi' de la putta?

> What's the matter, you son-of-a-bitch?   (I)

And the sonnet concludes:

> E che diavol sacc'io?

> How the hell do I know?   (I)

This is an entirely typical sampling of Angliolieri's particular level of diction, not obscene but quite appropriate for the lively and loud-voiced street scene which transpires.

The savorous *battibecco* between Cecco and Becchina beginning:

Becchina mia — Cecco, nol ti confesso   (XXII)

could not be further removed from the aulic elegancies of the *dolce stil nuovo*. Becchina, in particular, gives forth in shrill, plebian smart talk as she will on every succeeding appearance. Even the poet's church-minded mother, the *militissa,* in the few references which present-day scholarship accords her, appears as a pretty vulgar creature. Her putative greeting:

Cecco, va' che sie fenduto

Beat it, Cecco! May you be cut down   (LXXXV)

(Or in the current idiom, one might say "Drop dead!") scarcely presents her as a mistress of gentle speech. The poet's treatment of his father, replete with invective as we have already noted, is downright brutal. The few actual vulgarities are more amusing than shocking. We come upon such as:

Se tanto è savio, che curi le peta

If he is so smart, let him cure his own farting.   (LXVI)

In listing his meager possessions, he observes that he does have:

E mala letta per compier la danza

And an uncomfortable bed for a lover's jig.   (LXXI)

There are two or three allusions to the Straits of Messina, certainly with the intent of suggesting the genitalia, and a scattered phrase here and there, the meaning of which is no longer clear, but which appear to make some popular reference to sex. Yet sum total how innocent they are and devoid of pornography as we understand it today. Certainly there is none of the explicit smuttiness of Rustico, nor the occasionally scabrous details of a Catullus.

In terms of over-all craftsmanship and characteristic expression of his talents one can do no better than re-examine two or three of the better known sonnets. Let us consider firstly, *S'i' fosse foco,* which is by common consent one of his most effective. It has already been signaled briefly in passing in a different connection. Fabricated with a care which is not precisely the hallmark of Angiolieri, it stands apart, a model of construction, consistent in language, style and theme.

> S'i' fosse foco, arderei 'l mondo;
> s'i' fosse vento, lo tempesterei;
> s'i' fosse acqua, i' l'annegherei;
> s'i' fosse Dio, mandereil'en profondo;
>
> s'i fosse papa, sare' allor giocondo,
> ché tutti cristïani imbrigherei ;
> s'i' fosse 'mperator, sa' che farei?
> A tutti mozzarei lo capo a tondo.
>
> S'i' fosse morte, andarei da mio padre;
> s'i' fosse vita, fuggirei da lui:
> similemente farìa da mi' madre.
>
> S'i' fosse Cecco, com'i' sono e fui,
> torrei le donne giovani e leggiadre:
> e vecchie e laide lasserei altrui.

> If I were fire I'd burn the world away;
> If I were wind I'd turn my storms thereon;
> If I were water I'd soon let it drown;
> If I were God I'd sink it from the day;
> If I were Pope, I'd, never feel quite gay
> Until there was no peace beneath the sun;
> If I were Emperor, what would I have done?
> I'd lope men's heads all around in my own way.
> If I were Life I'd run away from him;
> And treat my mother to like calls and runs.
> If I were Cecco (and that's all my hope)
> I'd pick the nicest girls to suit my whim,
> And other folks should get the ugly ones.
>
> LXXXVI (Rossetti)

As Rho has observed, the essential merit of the sonnet is in its balance.[5] Straightway we sense the rage which impels Cecco, the flash of ugly misanthropy which cruelly illumines the first quatrain. In the second, his sense of the absurd begins subtly to alter the

---

[5] E. Rho, *Primitivi e romantici* (Firenze, 1937), p. 47.

tone. The suggested actions of a pope and a mad emperor are so preposterous as to make us smile. Then suddenly in the first tercet his dreadful attitude towards father and mother deliver another lethal blow; but before indignation can assert itself we are in the final tercet which is all smiles and fun. It is truly unique, this bizarre piece which ranges from the macabre to the frivolous. On second consideration we realize that it virtually sums up the poet in all the complexities and contradictions of his nature: infantilism, brilliance, rage and humor.

The rime scheme (abba abba cdc cdc) sets off the quatrains and tercets just sufficiently to emphasize the structure. Note furthermore how artfully the opening *S'i'fosse* is employed to introduce 10 of the 14 lines. It begins each line of the first quatrain, giving almost the effect that a drum might exercise in a martial passage, setting the tempo, arresting the attention. In the following it occurs only in alternate lines thus slightly retarding the march of the piece; subsequently twice in the first tercet where it is indispensable to contrast Death and Life; and finally, only in the first line of the last tercet. The total effect is much as though a composer had changed the tempo in a musical passage from 4/4 to 2/4 to 2/3 to 1/3.

The notoriety of this sonnet did much to foster the image of the *poète damné*. In this century, however, as soon as a more extensive sampling of his work became available, and a better notion of his true temperament emerged, the sonnet could be viewed as what it is, a frank "shocker" conceived to divert his public, which accustomed to his highly charged rhetoric, took it in its stride while appreciating, we trust, the finely wrought verse which it was their privilege to hear. If the hyperbolic tone strikes us as extreme today, it is well to recall, as Cavalli so rightly points out in his editorial notes, that the sonnet is in these respects entirely typical of the times, medieval in its images of pope, emperor, and cosmic phenomena, in its antitheses, as well as in the vivacity of its language and rythmn.

Angiolieri's remarkably felicitous handling of the dialogued sonnet has been commented upon particularly in relation to the saucy *battibecchi* between his lady-love and himself. The *Canzoniere* opens with perhaps the best of these, *Accorri, accorri, accorri, uom, a la strada*. In this a man, a passerby and a woman enact, each at the

STYLE AND TECHNIQUE 95

top of his lungs, in the middle of the street, this miniature drama. Are they Cecco, Becchina and an unknown? Very likely. But this time no names are mentioned and their noisy ordinariness rings with a universality that knows no time or place. In the translation the parts are indicated: (C) Cecco, (P) passerby, (D) woman (Becchina?) in conformity with present-day scholarship. Without identification of the participants in the trio, the sonnet is almost incomprehensible.

(C.) — Accorri accorri accorri, uom, a la strada!
(P.) — Che ha', fi' de la putta? (C.) — I' son rubato.
(P.) — Chi t'ha rubato? (C.) — Una che par che rada come rasoio, sì m'ha netto lasciato.

(P.) — Or come non le davi de la spada?
(C.) — I' dare' anz'a me. (P.) — Or se' 'mpazzato?
(C.) — Non so che 'l dà, così mi par che vada.
(P.) — Or travess'ella cieco, sciagurato!

(D.) — E vedi che ne pare a que' che 'l sanno?
(C.) — Di' quel che tu mi rubi. (D.) — Or va con Dio, ma anda pian, ch'i' vo' pianger lo danno,

ché ti diparti. (C.) — Con animo rio!
(D.) — Tu abbi 'l danno con tutto 'l malanno!
(C.) — Or chi m'ha morto? (D.) — E che diavol sacc'io?

(C) Help! come! help! you in the street!
(P) What's up, you son of a bitch? (C) I've been robbed!
(P) Who robbed you? (C) A girl who's snipped me
   Clean, like a razor, and left me bare.
(P) Well, why didn't you knife her?
(C) As well knife myself. (P) You must be crazy!
(C) It may be, but that's the way it is.
(P) She's really got you hooked — poor sucker!
(D) You see how it looks to those who know.
(C) Tell him what you've taken (D) Oh buzz off,
   But do it quietly so I can shed a tear
   Because you've gone. (C) In a black mood.
(D) It's your own fault you misery-lover.
(C) Well, who's laid me low? (D) Damned if I know. (I)

It is vulgar and human, and in its exaggerated emotions funny rather than sad despite the obvious distress of the main protagonist. What a far cry from the elegant and aristocratic milieux of Folgore di San Gemignano, and what an impudent caricature of the *dolce stil novo*! Yet what a relief from the oftentimes pallid and rarified sentiments of these latter! Cecco's sharp eye and ear had caught on numerous occasions just such little vignettes of street life in his native town. Note the liveliness of the language, the breathless impetus of the thrusts and sallies. There is not an excess word; in fact, some of the *répliques* are so astringent as to be cryptic. Ideally, the sonnet needs three interpretors to render the interplay of voices and moods since it is first of all a tiny playlet which Cecco with enormous skill has compressed into sonnet form. Originally Massera had assumed that only two persons were in colloqy. Difficulties in the manuscript and a complete absence of punctuation rendered the verse most difficult of interpretation. With the years and many readings the present version has emerged which probably represents what Angiolieri had actually written. Vittorio Rossi first sensed how much richer the scenario became if three speakers were involved, a view which is completely accepted today.[6]

This is Cecco at his characteristic best. The translation, alas, merely translates the cacaphony of their mean sentiments. The true savor is in the original. Observe again the Italian noting the rapid alternation of a's and o's which makes for the fluidity and speed of the sonnet. The rime scheme is simplicity itself: abab/abab/bcb/bcb but within the lines, an abundance of internal, or at least "echo" rimes maintains the nimble patter of the voices: strada - putta, rubato - rubato, una - rada, da - vada, danno - malanno. Cecco's ear is remarkably attuned to the musical pattern as the subtle interweaving of the sounds so amply attests.

A somewhat neglected sonnet, No. LII exhibits admirably in terms of content and structure the poets very considerable skill in weaving together a variety of themes into a compactly wrought verse, dressed as usual in smart and colorful language. His passion for Becchina is waning. She has betrayed him; but this time he is reasonable enough to see that the event has been providential since he has avoided the perilous reef of matrimony.

---

[6] Vide: *Giornale storico della letterature italiana* (1907), Vol. 49, pp. 389-90. Also: The excellent and persuasive article of A. Roncaglia, "Per due sonetti di di C. Angiolieri ed uno di Jacopo da Leona," *Giornale storico della letteratura italiana*, V. 98, 1941, p. 81 ff.

STYLE AND TECHNIQUE

 I' m'ho onde dar pace e debbo e voglio,
sed i' ho punto di ragion con meco;
po' ch'e' con la mia donna stat'è seco,
so che giammai non debbo sentir doglio.

 Di gioia mi vesto, di noia mi spoglio,
e ciò, ben ch'è 'n l'amor, a me' l'arreco;
ben posso dire: — Ave, Dominus tecò,
poi mi guardò di venir a lo scoglio;

 del quale i' era sì forte temente,
ch'a tutte l'ore, ch'i' a ciò pensava,
sì dardellava tutto a dente a dente,

 e non ch'altrui, ma me stess' odiava
Or moglie vo' com'i' odio 'l gaudente;
ma innanzi tratto ben so com'andava.

I can live in peace; I must and I will
If only there's a jot of reason in me.
Ever since that chap's been with my girl
I know that nevermore need I suffer grief.
I put on joy, I take off sorrow.
Tho' my love's been affronted, I'm the better for it
Well can I say, "Ave, Dominus tecum"
Since this has saved me from the reef
Of which I've been so fearful.
For every time I thought of it
My very teeth with terror chattered
Not only others but myself did I despise
I want a wife as much as I hate papa;
Well am I aware how things were going. (LII)

 Consider how neatly he has packaged within the unbelievable limits of 14 lines, autobiographical details, personal philosophizing, a bit of humor, a left-hand jab at his father, and withall has managed to emerge a little more mature and sensible than he has appeared at any time previous. Vitale in his *Rimatori comico e realistici del due e trecento* (p. 360) comments concerning the sonnet, that Cecco makes "of necessity a virtue." If, in the light of our acquaintance with the poet, the opening line with its "I must and I will" scarcely has the purposeful ring and fervor with which a Cornellian hero might invest it, at least it suggests incipient growth and reasonableness in Cecco which have been conspicuously lacking during this period of his infatuation.

The utter appropriateness of the simple, colloquial language is again lost in any literal translation which quite fails to convey the savor of the original, and savor is undeniably one of the most important ingredient's of the poet's work. Observe in this, for example, Cecco's expropriation for himself of the angel's words to Mary, "Ave, Dominus tecum," the reference not to "father" but to the (frate) gaudente, reminding his listeners that the despised skinflint took much pride in his membership in the prestigious society. The term gaudente "joyous" or "joyous reveler" is in itself an absurdity in its application to the father; note the amusing onomatopeia of *dardellava tutto a dente a dente*. The verses abound with unctuous o's which lend a certain oratorical flavor to the language. In short, the piece affords a perfect scenario for Cecco, the entertainer, besides exemplifying his outstanding skill as a sonnateer.

Negatively, Cecco, as has previously been charged, wants in spiritual quality and in nobility. His range of themes faults in its narrowness, the sentiments expressed are often demeaning. A similarity of passage, themes and even downright repetition detract from the slim legacy. If he scarcely polished and filed after the fashion of the Parnassians, is it not possible that some of the alleged repetitions may, in fact, represent development of the same theme for practice and experimentation. Is it not likely too that in reciting he altered and improvised, and that the written version may well have been taken down by another? Surely in the days before printing and typewriters the margin of error which occurred from one draft to another must have been considerable. Idle to speculate how the specific items turned up ultimately in what purported to be a fairly complete compilation of his work. If the laudable efforts of Todaro, Marti, Contini and others, abundantly signaled in earlier pages, have done much to tidy up the fascinating legacy, one cannot but wonder what might have been the results in arrangement, inclusion and deletion had circumstance and inclination permitted the author the privilege of editing his own work. In a moment of great artistic honesty, might he after the fashion of a Rouault, have consigned some to the fire, not that there are truly inferior pieces among them, merely that all are not of the same calibre. Perhaps he might even have contributed sonnets hithertoo unknown which would amuse and delight.

In terms of craftsmanship, today's reader may justifiably take issue with frequent lines which are so ellyptical as to occasion many paragraphs of exegetical comment and interpretation (Witness every edition from Massera to Vitale). Beyond a doubt some of these constitute simply sloppy transitions, makeshift *chevilles,* and hurried composition. The majority, however, must certainly represent allusions perfectly comprehensible to his contemporaries, though quite lost for us today, as well as idiomatic turns that have completely slipped from usage over the centuries. Another disconcerting stylistic feature which unfailingly strikes the modern eye is the multiplicity of lines which begin with the words: *e, ed, se, sed, ma, che, ched,* suggesting poverty of invention. Interestingly enough most of the verse of the comic and realistic school abounds in this practice, which apparently elicited no unfavorable reaction. Such, of course, is not the case with the poets of the *stil novo,* where a more elegant workmanship was the order of the day.

This is Cecco Angiolieri, one of the most original personalities in Italian letters; no great by any stretch of the imagination, indeed, one is tempted to observe that he often cuts a rather mean figure. Yet there are just enough intimations of greatness in his work to make him unforgetable. The words of de Musset apply quite aptly:

> Mon verre n'est pas grand
> Mais je bois dans mon verre.

Cecco is partially a product of his time; surely indebted both to those who went before as well as to his contemporaries, but the qualities which set him apart — as in the case of de Musset — are his and very typically his. The curious synthesis of sincerity and showmanship, the nearly indefinable humor which ranges from the unhinged to the raucous and flip, still exerts enormous appeal. In considerable measure he intrigues us because the element of speculation remains still paramount in any real assessment of him. One is never completely sure of him, never completely at ease with him. The artist commands admiration; the man alternately repels and attracts. The lack of any profundity in his work is virtually offset by splendid flights of technical brilliance. He rises head and shoulders above the fellow poets of his school, but stands lamentably below the great Florentine. We view him as darkly through a glass. The shadows of time obscure but never extinguish the effulgent flashes which remind us that this troubled but gifted Sienese left a *Canzoniere* which is one of the gems of the Middle Ages.

SELECTED BIBLIOGRAPHY

Angiolieri, Cecco. *Il Canzioniere* (Introduzione e commento di Carlo Steiner). Torino, 1928.
———. *Sonetti* (per cura di Aldo Francesco Massera). Bologna, 1906.
———. *Rime* (a cura di Gigi Cavalli). Milano, 1959.
Bartoli, Adolfo. *Storia della letteratura italiana*. Firenze, 1879.
Berrini, Nino. *Il Beffardo*. Milano, 1922.
Croce, Benedetto. *Poesia popolare e poesia d'arte*. Bari, 1933.
D'Ancona, A. *Studi di critica e storia letteraria*. Bologna, 1912.
Figurelli, Fernando. *La musa bizzarra di Cecco Angiolieri*. Napoli, 1950.
———. *La Poesia comico-giocosa dei primi due secoli*. Napoli, 1960.
Gardner, Edmund G. *The Story of Siena and San Gimignano*. London, 1904.
Gilasfurd, Alec. *Siena and the Hill Towns*. London, 1962.
LiGotti, Ettore. *Saggi*. Firenze, 1941.
Maier, Bruno. *La Personalità e la poesia di Cecco Angiolieri*. Bologna, 1947.
Marti, Mario. *Cultura e stile nei poeti giocosi del tempo di Dante*. Pisa, 1953.
Massera, Aldo Francesco. *Sonetti burleschi e realistici dei primi due secoli*. Bari, 1920.
Misciattelli, Piero. *The Mystics of Siena*. New York, 1930.
Nannetti, Elvira. *Cecco Angiolieri, La sua patria, i suoi tempi, e la sua poesia*. Siena, 1929.
Pirandello, Luigi. *Saggi*. Mondadori, 1939.
Sapegno, Natalino. *Il Trecento* (in: Storia Letteraria d'Italia). Milano, 1955.
Schevill, Ferdinand. Siena, *The History of a Medieval Commune*. New York, 1964.
Todaro, Adele. *Sull'autenticità dei sonetti attribuiti a Cecco Angiolieri*. Palermo, 1934.
Vitale, Maurizo. *Rimatori comico-realistici del due e trecento*. Torino, 1956.
Volpi, Guglielmo. *Il Trecento*. Milano (no date).

NORTH CAROLINA STUDIES IN THE ROMANCE LANGUAGES AND LITERATURES

I.S.B.N. Prefix 0-8078-

Recent Titles

C.-A. SAINTE-BEUVE. *Chateaubriand et son groupe littéraire sous l'empire.* Index alphabétique et analytique établi par Lorin A. Uffenbeck. 1973. (No 130). -930-8.

THE ORIGINS OF THE BAROQUE CONCEPT OF "PEREGRINATIO," by Juergen Hahn. 1973. (No. 131). -931-6.

THE "AUTO SACRAMENTAL" AND THE PARABLE IN SPANISH GOLDEN AGE LITERATURE, by Donald Thaddeus Dietz. 1973. (No. 132). -932-4.

FRANCISCO DE OSUNA AND THE SPIRIT OF THE LETTER, by Laura Calvert. 1973. (No. 133). -933-2.

ITINERARIO DI AMORE: DIALETTICA DI AMORE E MORTE NELLA VITA NUOVA, by Margherita de Bonfils Templer. 1973. (No. 134). -934-0.

L'IMAGINATION POETIQUE CHEZ DU BARTAS: ELEMENTS DE SENSIBILITE BAROQUE DANS LA "CREATION DU MONDE," by Bruno Braunrot. 1973. (No. 135). -934-0.

ARTUS DESIRE: PRIEST AND PAMPHLETEER OF THE SIXTEENTH CENTURY, by Frank S. Giese. 1973. (No. 136). -936-7.

JARDIN DE NOBLES DONZELLAS, FRAY MARTIN DE CORDOBA, by Harriet Goldberg. 1974. (No. 137). -937-5.

MYTHE ET PSYCHOLOGIE CHEZ MARIE DE FRANCE DANS "GUIGEMAR", par Antoinette Knapton. 1975. (No. 142). -942-1.

THE LYRIC POEMS OF JEHAN FROISSART: A CRITICAL EDITION, by Rob Roy McGregor, Jr. 1975. (No. 143). -943-X.

THE HISPANO-PORTUGUESE CANCIONERO OF THE HISPANIC SOCIETY OF AMERICA, by Arthur Askins. 1974. (No. 144). -944-8.

HISTORIA Y BIBLIOGRAFÍA DE LA CRÍTICA SOBRE EL "POEMA DE MÍO CID" (1750-1971), por Miguel Magnotta. 1976. (No. 145). -945-6.

LES ENCHANTEMENZ DE BRETAIGNE. AN EXTRACT FROM A THIRTEENTH CENTURY PROSE ROMANCE "LA SUITE DU MERLIN", edited by Patrick C. Smith. 1977. (No. 146). -9146-0.

THE DRAMATIC WORKS OF ÁLVARO CUBILLO DE ARAGÓN, by Shirley B. Whitaker. 1975. (No. 149). -949-9.

A CONCORDANCE TO THE "ROMAN DE LA ROSE" OF GUILLAUME DE LORRIS, by Joseph R. Danos. 1976. (No. 156). 0-88438-403-9.

POETRY AND ANTIPOETRY: A STUDY OF SELECTED ASPECTS OF MAX JACOB'S POETIC STYLE, by Annette Thau. 1976. (No. 158). -005-X.

FRANCIS PETRARCH, SIX CENTURIES LATER, by Aldo Scaglione. 1975. (No. 159).

STYLE AND STRUCTURE IN GRACIÁN'S "EL CRITICÓN", by Marcia L. Welles, 1976. (No. 160). -007-6.

MOLIERE: TRADITIONS IN CRITICISM, by Laurence Romero. 1974 (Essays, No. 1). -001-7.

CHRÉTIEN'S JEWISH GRAIL. A NEW INVESTIGATION OF THE IMAGERY AND SIGNIFICANCE OF CHRÉTIEN DE TROYES'S GRAIL EPISODE BASED UPON MEDIEVAL HEBRAIC SOURCES, by Eugene J. Weinraub. 1976. (Essays, No. 2). -002-5.

FIRE AND ICE: THE POETRY OF XAVIER VILLAURRUTIA, by Merlin H. Forster. 1976. (Essays, No. 11). -011-4.

THE THEATER OF ARTHUR ADAMOV, by John J. McCann. 1975. (Essays, No. 13). -013-0.

AN ANATOMY OF POESIS: THE PROSE POEMS OF STÉPHANE MALLARMÉ, by Ursula Franklin. 1976. (Essays, No. 16). -016-5.

When ordering please cite the *ISBN Prefix* plus the last four digits for each title.

Send orders to: University of North Carolina Press
Chapel Hill
North Carolina 27514
U. S. A.

NORTH CAROLINA STUDIES IN THE ROMANCE LANGUAGES AND LITERATURES

I.S.B.N. Prefix 0-8078-

Recent Titles

LAS MEMORIAS DE GONZALO FERNÁNDEZ DE OVIEDO, Vols. I and II, by Juan Bautista Avalle-Arce. 1974. (Texts, Textual Studies, and Translations, Nos. 1 and 2). *-401-2; 402-0.*

GIACOMO LEOPARDI: THE WAR OF THE MICE AND THE CRABS, translated, introduced and annotated by Ernesto G. Caserta. 1976. (Texts, Textual Studies, and Translations, No. 4). *-404-7.*

LUIS VÉLEZ DE GUEVARA: A CRITICAL BIBLIOGRAPHY, by Mary G. Hauer. 1975. (Texts, Textual Studies, and Translations, No. 5). *-405-5.*

UN TRÍPTICO DEL PERÚ VIRREINAL: "EL VIRREY AMAT, EL MARQUÉS DE SOTO FLORIDO Y LA PERRICHOLI". EL "DRAMA DE DOS PALANGANAS" Y SU CIRCUNSTANCIA, estudio preliminar, reedición y notas por Guillermo Lohmann Villena. 1976. (Texts, Textual Studies, and Translation, No. 15). *-415-2.*

LOS NARRADORES HISPANOAMERICANOS DE HOY, edited by Juan Bautista Avalle-Arce. 1973. (Symposia, No. 1). *-951-0.*

ESTUDIOS DE LITERATURA HISPANOAMERICANA EN HONOR A JOSÉ J. ARROM, edited by Andrew P. Debicki and Enrique Pupo-Walker. 1975. (Symposia, No. 2). *-952-9.*

MEDIEVAL MANUSCRIPTS AND TEXTUAL CRITICISM, edited by Christopher Kleinhenz. 1976. (Symposia, No. 4). *-954-5.*

SAMUEL BECKETT. THE ART OF RHETORIC, edited by Edouard Morot-Sir, Howard Harper, and Dougald McMillan III. 1976. (Symposia, No. 5). *-955-3.*

DELIE. CONCORDANCE, by Jerry Nash. 1976. 2 Volumes. (No. 174).

FIGURES OF REPETITION IN THE OLD PROVENÇAL LYRIC: A STUDY IN THE STYLE OF THE TROUBADOURS, by Nathaniel B. Smith. 1976. (No. 176). *-9176-2.*

A CRITICAL EDITION OF LE REGIME TRESUTILE ET TRESPROUFITABLE POUR CONSERVER ET GARDER LA SANTE DU CORPS HUMAIN, by Patricia Willett Cummins. 1977. (No. 177).

THE DRAMA OF SELF IN GUILLAUME APOLLINAIRE'S "ALCOOLS", by Richard Howard Stamelman. 1976. (No. 178). *-9178-9.*

A CRITICAL EDITION OF "LA PASSION NOSTRE SEIGNEUR" FROM MANUSCRIPT 1131 FROM THE BIBLIOTHEQUE SAINTE-GENEVIEVE, PARIS, by Edward J. Gallagher. 1976. (No. 179). *-9179-7.*

A QUANTITATIVE AND COMPARATIVE STUDY OF THE VOCALISM OF THE LATIN INSCRIPTIONS OF NORTH AFRICA, BRITAIN, DALMATIA, AND THE BALKANS, by Stephen William Omeltchenko. 1977. (No. 180). *-9180-0.*

OCTAVIEN DE SAINT-GELAIS "LE SEJOUR D'HONNEUR", edited by Joseph A. James. 1977. (No. 181). *-9181-9.*

A STUDY OF NOMINAL INFLECTION IN LATIN INSCRIPTIONS, by Paul A. Gaeng. 1977. (No. 182). *-9182-7.*

THE LIFE AND WORKS OF LUIS CARLOS LÓPEZ, by Martha S. Bazik. 1977. (No. 183). *-9183-5.*

"THE CORT D'AMOR". A THIRTEENTH-CENTURY ALLEGORICAL ART OF LOVE, by Lowanne E. Jones. 1977. (No. 185). *-9185-1.*

PHYTONYMIC DERIVATIONAL SYSTEMS IN THE ROMANCE LANGUAGES: STUDIES IN THEIR ORIGIN AND DEVELOPMENT, by Walter E. Geiger. 1978. (No. 187). *-9187-8.*

LANGUAGE IN GIOVANNI VERGA'S EARLY NOVELS, by Nicholas Patruno. 1977. (No. 188). *-9188-6.*

When ordering please cite the *ISBN Prefix* plus the last four digits for each title.

Send orders to: University of North Carolina Press
Chapel Hill
North Carolina 27514
U. S. A.

NORTH CAROLINA STUDIES IN THE ROMANCE LANGUAGES AND LITERATURES

I.S.B.N. Prefix 0-8078-

Recent Titles

BLAS DE OTERO EN SU POESÍA, by Moraima de Semprún Donahue. 1977. (No. 189). -9189-4.

LA ANATOMÍA DE "EL DIABLO COJUELO": DESLINDES DEL GÉNERO ANATOMÍSTICO, por C. George Peale. 1977. (No. 191). -9191-6.

RICHARD SANS PEUR, EDITED FROM "LE ROMANT DE RICHART" AND FROM GILLES CORROZET'S "RICHART SANS PAOUR", by Denis Joseph Conlon. 1977. (No. 192). -9192-4.

MARCEL PROUST'S GRASSET PROOFS. *Commentary and Variants*, by Douglas Alden. 1978. (No. 193). -9193-2.

MONTAIGNE AND FEMINISM, by Cecile Insdorf. 1977. (No. 194). -9194-0.

SANTIAGO F. PUGLIA, AN EARLY PHILADELPHIA PROPAGANDIST FOR SPANISH AMERICAN INDEPENDENCE, by Merle S. Simmons. 1977. (No. 195). -9195-9.

BAROQUE FICTION-MAKING. A STUDY OF GOMBERVILLE'S "POLEXANDRE", by Edward Baron Turk. 1978. (No. 196). -9196-7.

THE TRAGIC FALL: DON ÁLVARO DE LUNA AND OTHER FAVORITES IN SPANISH GOLDEN AGE DRAMA, by Raymond R. MacCurdy. 1978. (No. 197). -9197-5.

A BAHIAN HERITAGE. An Ethnolinguistic Study of African Influences on Bahian Portuguese, by William W. Megenney. 1978. (No. 198). -9198-3.

"LA QUERELLE DE LA ROSE: Letters and Documents", by Joseph L. Baird and John R. Kane. 1978. (No. 199). -9199-1.

TWO AGAINST TIME. *A Study of the very present worlds of Paul Claudel and Charles Péguy*, by Joy Nachod Humes. 1978. (No. 200). -9200-9.

TECHNIQUES OF IRONY IN ANATOLE FRANCE. Essay on *Les sept femmes de la Barbe-Bleue*, by Diane Wolfe Levy. 1978. (No. 201). -9201-7.

THE PERIPHRASTIC FUTURES FORMED BY THE ROMANCE REFLEXES OF "VADO (AD)" "PLUS INFINITIVE, by James Joseph Champion. 1978 (No. 202). -9202-5.

THE EVOLUTION OF THE LATIN /b/-/ʋ/ MERGER: A Quantitative and Comparative Analysis of the *B-V* Alternation in Latin Inscriptions, by Joseph Louis Barbarino. 1978 (No. 203). -9203-3.

METAPHORIC NARRATION: THE STRUCTURE AND FUNCTION OF METAPHORS IN "A LA RECHERCHE DU TEMPS PERDU", by Inge Karalus Crosman. 1978 (No. 204). -9204-1.

LE VAIN SIECLE GUERPIR. A Literary Approach to Sainthood through Old French Hagiography of the Twelfth Century, by Phyllis Johnson and Brigitte Cazelles. 1979. (No. 205). -9205-X.

THE POETRY OF CHANGE: A STUDY OF THE SURREALIST WORKS OF BENJAMIN PÉRET, by Julia Field Costich. 1979. (No. 206). -9206-8.

NARRATIVE PERSPECTIVE IN THE POST-CIVIL WAR NOVELS OF FRANCISCO AYALA "MUERTES DE PERRO" AND "EL FONDO DEL VASO", by Maryellen Bieder. 1979. (No. 207). -9207-6.

RABELAIS: HOMO LOGOS, by Alice Fiola Berry. 1979. (No. 208). -9208-4.

"DUEÑAS" AND "DONCELLAS": A STUDY OF THE "DOÑA RODRÍGUEZ" EPISODE IN "DON QUIJOTE", by Conchita Herdman Marianella. 1979. (No. 209). -9209-2.

PIERRE BOAISTUAU'S "HISTOIRES TRAGIQUES": A STUDY OF NARRATIVE FORM AND TRAGIC VISION, by Richard A. Carr. 1979. (No. 210). -9210-6.

THE FICTIONS OF THE SELF. THE EARLY WORKS OF MAURICE BARRES, by Gordon Shenton. 1979. (No. 214). -9214-9.

CECCO ANGIOLIERI. A STUDY, by Gifford P. Orwen. 1979. (No. 215). -9215-7.

When ordering please cite the *ISBN Prefix* plus the last four digits for each title.

Send orders to: University of North Carolina Press
                  Chapel Hill
                  North Carolina 27514
                  U. S. A.

The Department of Romance Studies Digital Arts and Collaboration Lab at the University of North Carolina at Chapel Hill is proud to support the digitization of the North Carolina Studies in the Romance Languages and Literatures series.

www.ingramcontent.com/pod-product-compliance
Lightning Source LLC
Chambersburg PA
CBHW020421230426
43663CB00007BA/1258